Ragtime Blues

Oak Anthology of Blues Guitar

Ragtime Blues

By Stefan Grossman

Oak Publications
New York • London • Sydney

Photo Credits

Doug Connor	12
Georges Chatelain	36
Lewis Kahn	50
David Gahr	53
George Mitchell	62
Herbert Wise	68
Leslie Bauman	85, 93

Photo Captions

Blind Lemon Jefferson	22
Blind Willie McTell	32
Rev. Gary Davis	36
Blind Boy Fuller	43
Big Bill Broonzy	54, 57
Blind Blake	80

Soundsheet Contents

Side One
Blind Lemon Jefferson
    Hot Dogs
    Easy Rider Blues
    Black Horse Blues
Blind Willie McTell
    Stole Rider Blues
William Moore
    One Way Gal
Blind Boy Fuller
    Piccolo Rag

Side Two
Blind Blake
    West Coast Blues
    That Will Never Happen No More
    Police Dog Blues
Sam McGee
    Franklin Blues
Blind Blake
    Policy Blues
Blind Boy Fuller
    Careless Love

Cover design by Tim Metevier
Book design by Nina Clayton
Edited by Brook Hedick and Peter Pickow

Copyright © 1970, 1984 by Oak Publications,
A Division of Embassy Music Corporation, New York, NY.

International Standard Book Number: 0.8256.0118.5
Library of Congress Catalog Card Number: 76-113474

Exclusive Distributors:
Music Sales Corporation
24 East 22nd Street, New York, NY 10010 USA
Music Sales Limited
8/9 Frith Street, London W1V 5TZ England
Music Sales Pty. Limited
120 Rothschild Street, Rosebery, Sydney, NSW 2018, Australia

Printed in the United States of America by
Vicks Lithograph and Printing Corporation

About the Author

I first met Stefan Grossman some years ago while playing at Gerde's Folk City. At that time he was a young and enthusiastic teenager dogging the footsteps of his first teacher and mentor, Rev. Gary Davis; and, it seemed, relishing his historically romantic role as "lead boy" to the great street singer and guitarist. His eyes and ears were devouring the songs and styles of Rev. Davis, and it wasn't long before he could recreate his most complex arrangements.

Stefan didn't stop there (an accomplishment in itself), but went on to study, in depth, the guitar styles of other Country blues singers, using as his source material an extensive tape and record collection. He always transferred what he learned to the guitar, and learned to play the intricate blues styles of Mississippi, Alabama, Texas, and North Carolina. Some of his accomplishments in this field can be heard on his Kicking Mule instruction record *How To Play Blues Guitar*, as well as in the transcriptions in this book.

Although his first and foremost love has always been Country blues, Stefan's creative musicianship has brought him into a variety of musical roles, from playing ragtime guitar in the legendary "Even Dozen Jug Band" to lead guitar in the highly amplified "Fugs" and "Chicago Loop." In the summer of 1967 Stefan went to England, and was in immediate demand in clubs, concert halls, and recording studios there.

From reports that have reached this side of the Atlantic, he is now recording and performing songs of his own composition, as well as traditional American music, and has been received with warmth and enthusiasm wherever he has played.

HAPPY TRAUM

Preface

There are many intellectual curiosities about the blues. It has always seemed a phenomenon that the guitar styles that came out of the South during the twenties and thirties could be differentiated by their regional characteristics. On hearing a strange new artist, one can almost pinpoint his city of origin through his guitar technique. The Mississippi Delta produced a sound distinct from that of Texas. Atlanta had a very popular style that seems to have been confined to that city. The music of Louisiana has a weird voodoo texture, while the Carolinas produced another totally different sound.

The list can be lengthened and more adjectives can be invented to explain the music. But we are at a disadvantage, in that what we can talk about is limited historically and defined only by the recorded picture. We can speak only about those artists who made records and not the hundreds who seem to have been forgotten. The last years have seen the rediscovery of many artists who were, and still are, the greats in their field of blues. It is also impossible to determine whether the artist came first or the style. Some artists were very popular and were imitated throughout the South. Their records, as well as live performances, spread their sounds and one can presume that in their travels they were influenced by other styles.

But I suppose this gets a little ethereal even though it is interesting. What is important is what has remained. I have explored the styles of Mississippi and Memphis in *Delta Blues* and *Country Blues* published by Oak. One was a very hard blues and the other a happy-sounding imitation of piano based on an alternating bass guitar style. These two styles are very different in right-hand techniques and in their approaches to making up arrangements.

This volume deals with a group of Ragtime bluesmen—men who played blues as well as Ragtime songs—men from different parts of the South, with nothing in common except the type of music they picked to record.

Blind Lemon Jefferson was from Texas. William Moore was from Virginia. Blind Willie McTell was from Georgia and was last heard playing somewhere in New Jersey! Blind Boy Fuller was a native of Durham, North Carolina. Big Bill Broonzy was from Mississippi and spent the latter part of his life in Chicago. Blind Blake was from Tampa, Florida. So regionally, these artists had little in common. They were perhaps the most popular race artists of their time, with the possible exception of the classic female blues singers and Lonnie Johnson. Of all of them, Blind Blake seems to have had the greatest guitar influence. He was the "governor." His style was copied throughout the South. His records seem to have been the "trend setters" for the young guitarists. A gentleman like Rev. Gary Davis who never met Blake can remember note for note a dozen Blake pieces. Rev. Davis taught many pupils, the most famous being Blind Boy Fuller. You can see how the learning process spreads an individual's "sounds." Fuller and Broonzy both simplified Blake's complicated guitar style to produce their own. Both of these men were very popular recording artists and their work shows a great range of ideas that were never included in Blake's recorded works.

Blind Lemon Jefferson seems to be somewhat isolated from the others. He also had an enormous popularity. His old discs number close to the hundred mark. His guitar style is quite unique. It is rhythmically different from the others mentioned in this book. Lemon didn't seem to concentrate on instrumentals but instead on the presentation of his songs. Some pieces imitate the old boogie-woogie piano while others are just straight dance tunes or blues. But in all of his songs he put in something different that distinguishes his work from all others. Whether this was done so guitarists would find it hard to imitate or whether he heard the music that way, we shall never know.

Blind Lemon's sound is probably the oldest of those mentioned in this volume, and relates closer to primitive African sounds and rhythms than most of the other ragtime-oriented guitarists.

All of these artists combined the alternating bass technique with a technique of playing treble melody lines without bass notes. They also complicated and explored the alternating bass by half-timing or double-timing it. This makes the guitar sound closer yet to the ragtime piano, which popularized the stop-time and Charleston beat.

I have tried to give a broad view of the type of songs these men did. Presented in this volume are a large number of selections exploring the different keys and tunings used. This book will help further the study begun in *Country Blues*. Here we take the same stylistic approach explained in that book and explore it further.

The only major person omitted from this study is Rev. Gary Davis. He taught me much of what I know in this style. He has developed an incredible, unique sound using the same ideas mentioned in this book. His many different approaches to music can be found in the Oak publication *Rev. Gary Davis/Blues and Rags*.

The discography for this volume is very important and based on approximately eight records. Try to hear these if possible as the accenting of the notes is something that can never be expressed satisfactorily in tablature or music.

There are some very happy sounds in this book and I hope you enjoy them.

STEFAN GROSSMAN

Contents

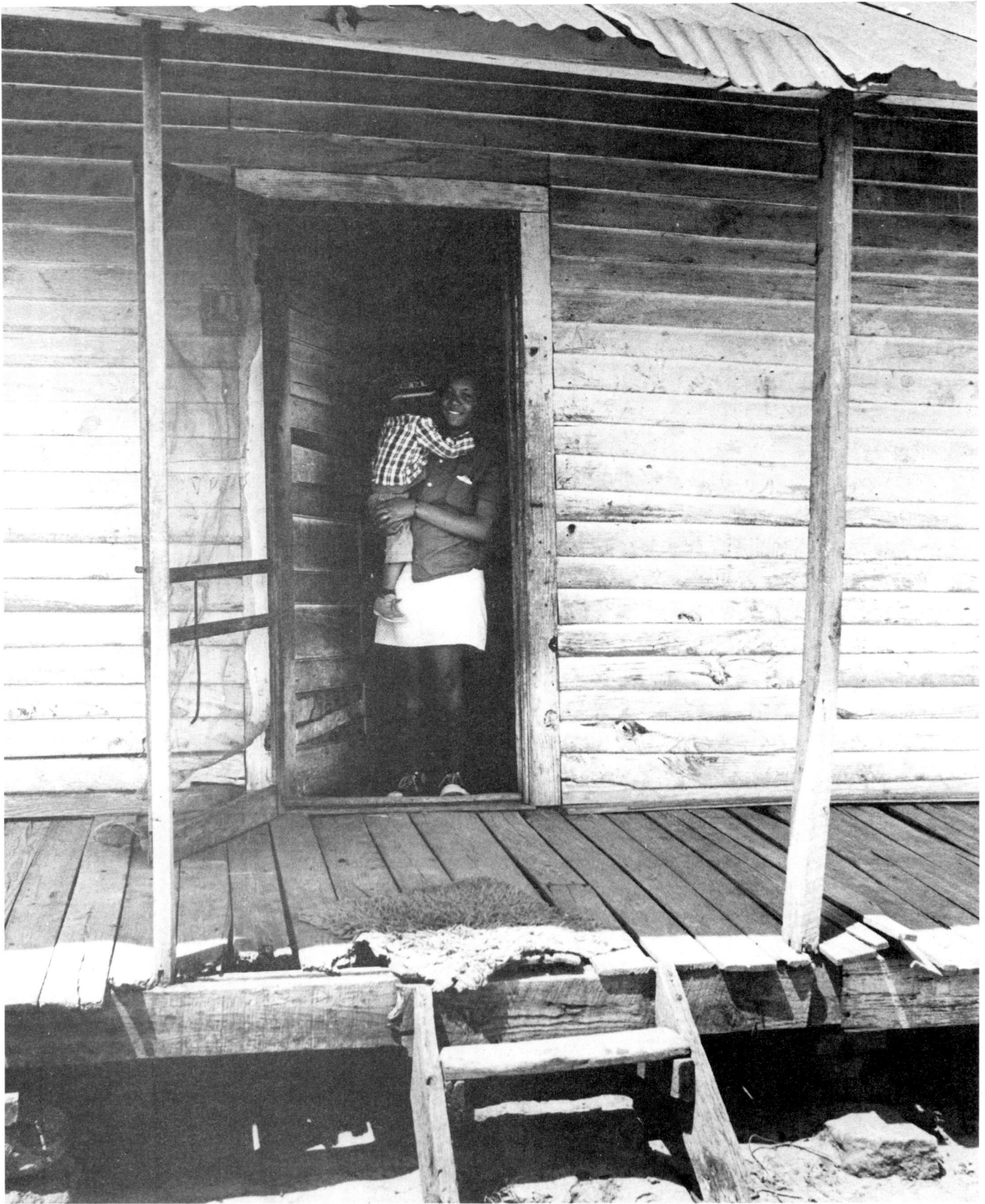

Introduction

"Objective music is all based on 'inner octaves'. And it can obtain not only definite psychological results but definite physical results. There can be such music as would freeze water. There can be such music as would kill a man instantaneously. The Biblical legend of the destruction of the walls of Jericho by music is precisely a legend of objective music. Plain music, no matter of what kind, will not destroy walls, but objective music indeed can do so. And not only can it destroy but it can also build up. In the legend of Orpheus there are hints of objective music, for Orpheus used to impart knowledge by music. Snake charmers' music in the East is an approach to objective music, of course very primitive. Very often it is simply one note which is long drawn out, rising and falling only very little; but in this single note 'inner octaves' are going on all the time and melodies of 'inner octaves' which are inaudible to the ears but felt by the emotional center. And the snake hears this music or, more strictly speaking, he feels it, and obeys it. The same music, only a little more complicated, and men would obey it."

From the teachings of G.I. Gurdjieff

I remember seeing Son House at the Gaslight Cafe in New York City. He had just been rediscovered and was still quite nervous to play before people. He slowly rambled up to the stage and took a seat. The lights were bright and made it almost impossible for him to see the audience. Next, the steel guitar was handed to him and he fumbled to get a brass piece of tubing from his vest pocket. The Cafe was full of noise and excitement. There was little recognition of Son's being on stage. Then, to quiet the place, an announcement was made introducing the "legendary bluesman from the Mississippi Delta." Still noise, as most of the audience were very unfamiliar with Delta music or Son House.

Then the amazing part of the night occurred. Son slid the slide down the fingerboard of the guitar. The sound cried out. Everyone stood and looked. Next Son started his singing moan. His eyes rolled, arms shook, sweat quickly rolled down his forehead. Everyone remained standing, amazed at the sound. The song ended and from stunned silence a wave of applause emerged. Son played four more songs. The blues brought tears to people who had never been exposed to this type of sound. Those familiar with Son and his music cried for the joy of seeing him perform and from the wailing sounds of the guitar.

Music is quite a powerful tool. Words of explanation can never express the impact of a musical experience. I am going to attempt to teach the music of some great guitar bluesmen. It is not going to be isolated and picked apart but presented with its historical value as well as personal and emotional value. Words will not be my tools for this venture; instead I will incorporate photographs, interviews, and records to describe these feelings.

The important part of this learning process remains in your hands. You must hear the records and performances of the people mentioned. Many are dead, others are alive and still performing.

From 1962 to 1970, I lived with and learned from Rev. Gary Davis, Mississippi John Hurt, Son House, Skip James, Fred McDowell, and Mance Lipscomb. All these men patiently explained their music in terms of their life and times.

Other bluesmen who were just names on old 78s were revealed as real people. All of these musicians helped to formulate an American style of playing music on the acoustic guitar.

During the twenties and thirties these men were recorded by small record companies. When The Depression hit, the record business collapsed. Their music was presented as "race music." Music for the Negro race. After forty years this music has become accepted and played by the whites, as well as being continued by many blacks. Who would have thought in 1930 that a record like "I'm So Glad" would ever find its way into the homes of millions of people. When Skip James first issued this record on the Paramount Record Company label only a few dozen were sold. Forty-five years after its first release, Skip was able to watch the group *Cream* perform and record this tune.

I would like to thank Pete Whalen, Bernie Klatzsko, Pete Kaufman, Richard Spottswood, Nick Perls, and Larry Cohn for making available their many rare old 78s. Together we have spent many hours listening to and discussing these old records.

For the many wonderful photographs used throughout this series I would like to thank Dick Waterman, Pete Whalen, Larry Cohn, Sam and Ann Charters, Chris Strachweiz, Herbert Grossman, Jack Prelutsky, Christine Brown and Georges Chatelain.

I have not attempted to delve into detailed discographical explanations of the individual songs presented. My main aim is to present guitar styles and techniques. I hope that these books will serve that purpose. For those interested in the history or discussions on the Country blues I suggest you see Sam Charter's *The Bluesmen* or Stephen Calt's introduction to the *Country Blues Songbook* (out of print). Over the last years a wealth of material has been published concerning the lives of bluesmen and these can be found through the blues magazine *Blues Unlimited* (38A Sackville Road, Bexhill-on-Sea, Sussex, England).

The *Anthology of Blues Guitarists* will have five volumes. The first deals with Mississippi John Hurt and the Memphis sound, *Country Blues*. The second volume is a study into the music of the Mississippi Delta, *Delta Blues*. The third book deals with various ragtime blues guitarists, i.e. Blind Blake, Blind Lemon Jefferson, Blind Boy Fuller and Big Bill Broonzy,

Ragtime Blues. The fourth is a study into the blues and ragtime techniques of Rev. Gary Davis, *Rev. Gary Davis/Blues and Rags*. The fifth volume will discuss the blues styles of Texas, *Texas Blues*.

Hopefully all five volumes will stand as one. It is my hope that these books will help document the various regional acoustic blues guitar techniques and to show that a unique way of playing the guitar has been developed in America. A way of playing the guitar that is just as valid, exciting, and detailed as the Classical or any other method.

The study of these styles is not a spoon-feeding process. It will require much of your time and involvement. The end result will allow you to play many styles of Country Blues. It is my hope that from there you will go on to develop your own sound, style, and techniques. You must listen to the various records and tapes available of the material presented.

This music has been a great part of my life. I hope some of the excitement I've found in it can be shared with you.

Peace,

STEFAN GROSSMAN

The Tablature System

At an early age I began to play music. The formality and coldness of the teaching methods as well as the dull material brought a quick end to my interest. The printed music page seemed a strange and difficult language to master. Furthermore, who was interested in *Autumn Leaves* or *Tea for Two*? The songs had no personal appeal for me. Years later I once again picked up a guitar and started to play. This time I wisely shied away from organized music theory. Sounds from my head found their way to the guitar. I concentrated on playing and not learning about sharps, flats, time signatures, key changes and chord structures. I didn't want to be cramped by words. A few months after this departure from convention, I was sitting before, and learning from, Rev. Gary Davis.

For two years I concentrated on the many styles Rev. Davis patiently taught me. I spent hours up at his house breathing in thick cigar smoke, eating Mrs. Davis's cooking and learning incredible songs. From this experience I devised a method for writing down the material. I needed this so that I could learn and remember more in a lesson.

So instead of two songs a day I was able to absorb five. The system I developed showed only the fret positions of the strings. The sound, rhythm, and accent of the piece was all in my head. My system depended on hearing the song. The chord positions were drawn or rather scribbled out so that no fingering problems would arise.

The tablature presented here is a culmination and a neater version of that developed at Rev. Davis's house. It still helps to hear the piece of music. All of the items being taught are available on either record or tape. The sources are all listed in the discography at the end of the book.

To me tablature is intended for those people who want to learn how to play first and learn the theory second. In this type of "primitive" music, theory can become very involved since there were no rules. The artist did what he wanted how he wanted on his instrument. This feeling is hopefully continued in the spirit of the tablature. It is to help you only to find the notes. The records will give you the feel. You then are left to put the song together. No mat-

ter what, it will come out unique! Your fingers are yours. Your touch is yours. These are unique and will develop your own sound no matter how hard you try to imitate other players.

Now, to the tablature.

Each horizontal line indicates a string. The treble strings are on the top and the bass strings are on the bottom.

A number on any line indicates the fretted position. A zero would mean to play an open string. A one would indicate that that string would be pressed down at the first fret. Take for instance the diagram below. The zero is on the second string and thus means that the open second string is played. The one is placed on the third string's space and means that you would play the third string pressed down at the first fret. Likewise, the four indicates fourth string, fourth fret.

In all of these volumes we will concern ourselves with fingerpicking guitar styles. This is generally done by playing with the thumb, index, and middle fingers of the right hand (presuming that you are a righty). To show this we use stems going up and down from the numbers showing fretted positions. A stem down means that the thumb strikes the note. If the stem is up, your index or middle finger strikes the note. In this case I leave it to your comfort. Use either finger. This clarifies itself when a song is played up to tempo. The diagram below shows an open sixth string being played with the thumb and then the second fret of the third string played with the index finger.

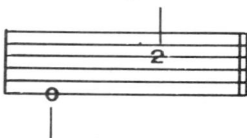

In most cases the thumb will play an alternating bass usually on the three bass strings. The index and middle finger will play notes on the first, second, and third string. But again these aren't rules and there are many exceptions.

When fingerpicking one has two choices: You either can pinch two notes together or not. A pinch is also called a pluck in some books. It will be obvious when two notes (numbers) are to be pinched because they will be perfectly aligned vertically, along with their stems. Pinches may occasionally include two or three treble notes along with the bass note.

In the above example we have, from left to right, the following: first, the open sixth string is played by the thumb; next, the sixth string, first fret is pinched together with the third string, third fret. The sixth string is plucked with the thumb, and the third with the index finger. Next, the thumb strikes the third fret of the fourth string. This is similar to an alternating bass pattern. The next notes are played with the thumb on the sixth string, first fret. This is pinched with two notes in the treble. The index and middle finger strike the first string, first fret, and the second string, third fret. The next note is played with the index finger hitting the second string, first fret. Lastly we have the bass note played with the thumb on the fourth string, third fret.

Many times in blues playing, the notes are not articulated precisely. In these cases, the stems have been used mainly to show the overall rhythm. This is often accompanied by arrows that indicate that the strings should be "brushed." Once again, the notation and technique will make sense as the song is played.

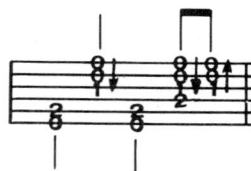

In the first part of the example, the thumb hits the open sixth string but the fifth string. second fret sounds also. This is done by just playing harder on the sixth string. The force will

make the fifth string vibrate. This technique can be done in the treble as well as the bass. Next we see an arrow. This indicates a brush. If the arrow points up, the hand brushes up toward the sixth string. If down, the hand brushes down to the first string. The number of strings to be affected is indicated by the length of the arrow. For instance, the next group of notes shows a brush up towards the sixth string on the open first, open second and third string, first fret. Next is the open sixth string with the vibrating fifth. Then an arrow that shows that we brush up towards the sixth string but this time the fourth string, second fret vibrates. It is not hit but is affected by the other three notes. This effect is gotten by damping the strings with your right-hand palm or with an upward stroke of the right hand. This sound is difficult to explain. But in many pieces you can hear notes sounding yet you know that they are not being hit. This is the nature of the guitar. By hitting one string it will set other strings to vibrate. The last notes in this example are a brush down to the open first, second, and the third string, first fret.

The example given above would most likely be accompanied by a letter indicating what chord is being used.

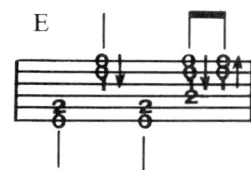

There are certain effects used in blues guitar that are also symbolized in the tablature.

The first shown is a *hammer-on.* Here, the number of the fret to be "hammered" is placed to the right of the curved line and is accompanied by the letter "H." The result is two different sounds executed with one right-hand stroke. The next effect is a *wham* or a bent note. This is designated with a "W." In this example, the second string is to be "whammed" (bent upward) at the eighth fret, while the first string is played at the seventh fret. These two sounds are played with the index and middle fingers respectively. The dot next to the number (not the stem) represents a harmonic played first with the index finger on the third string, twelfth fret; then with the thumb on the fourth string, twelfth fret. *Slides* are shown with a dash. In this example, you would slide along the sixth string from the second to the fourth fret; once again executing two different sounds with only one right-hand thumb-stroke. The last example is of a *pull-off.* Like a hammer-on, this is represented by a curved line, and is accompanied by the letter "P." The open fifth string is pinched together with the second string pressed down at the ninth fret, which is pulled-off hard enough to sound the second string at the seventh fret.

This all sounds wordy and complicated, but once you become familiar with the tablature it will all become very simple and automatic. All of my students end up sight-reading the tablature. As for tonality and accent, this is left for you to hear in the original record.

The pieces have been arranged by artist, and not by difficulty. You may find a simple song in the middle of the book, and sometimes a hard one near the beginning. This is to stagger your development. You learn a few simple pieces and then slow down your learning process with a hard one. By the end of the volume you will have explored all the keys that that style is played in.

You should be familiar with the terms used so far. If not, just glance at a beginner's folk guitar book. This will help you to define the terms. The books in the *Anthology of Blues Guitarists* have material ranging from beginners' pieces to those challenging to even an advanced guitar player. It is especially designed for those sincerely interested in learning blues guitar techniques. The end result, however, will allow you to play pop, folk, rock or jazz. This belief comes from my own learning experience.

I have a record on the Kicking Mule label entitled *How to Play Blues Guitar* (109). This could answer some of your questions if they should arise.

If there are any other queries please feel free to contact me through Oak Publications. I will be more than glad to clear up any problems.

Good luck and enjoy. You have lots of good music before you.

STEFAN GROSSMAN

Bilingual Notation System
Tablature and Standard Music

In order to facilitate learning the pieces in this collection, we have written them out in both *tablature* and *standard music* notation. The two systems are shown simultaneously, line-by-line, with standard music above and tablature below.

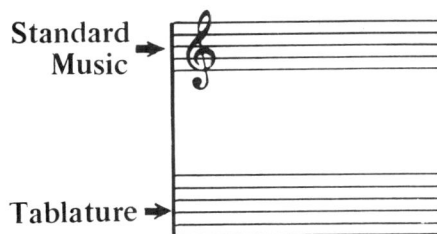

Stems

As you can see by examining the songs, our use of stems in the tablature corresponds very closely with its counterpart in the standard music directly above it.

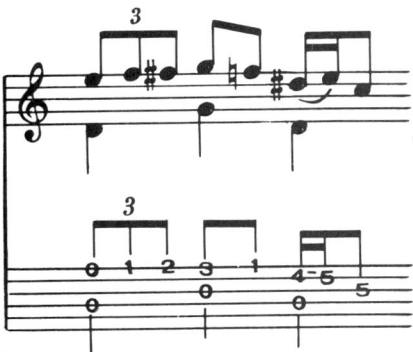

As is evident from the example above, the stems serve two functions:

(1) to indicate whether a given note is to be played by the thumb (downward stem ⌐) or by either index or middle finger (upward stem ♩);

(2) to represent the rhythm which is to be played; i.e., the exact combination of individual note values (lengths) and groupings of notes and silences into phrases which are unique to that song.

Rhythm and Time Values

Rhythm is a language comprised of units of time. The duration of a sound or a silence is designated by different kinds of *notes* or *rests*, respectively. In both standard music notation and tab, larger, regular rhythmic units are grouped into *measures* (or *bars*) that are set apart from each other by vertical *bar lines*.

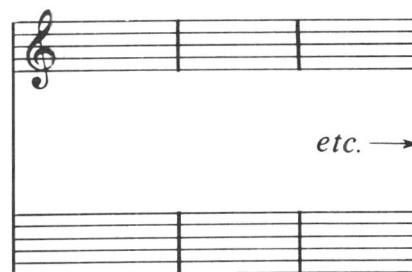

Each note or rest in any measure exists for a specific length of time. These time values relate to all other notes and rests in the measure or piece. Each of the symbols that represent the various relative lengths of time for which a note is held, also has a counterpart symbol which represents the same length for which there is to be a silence (represented by rests).

Just as the English language is a system which conveys ideas through an alphabet of letters and punctuations, Western music is conveyed through an alphabet of notes (letters) showing pitch and pitch length, and rests (punctuations) showing pauses, silences, etc.

Differences between Music and Tablature

The reader will notice some differences between music and tab that may seem incongruous at first glance, especially in the notation of rhythmic values. However, these differences arise for purely practical rather than technical reasons: they keep the tablature pleasant to read and

NOTE VALUES

Tablature	Standard Music
2, 2 2 (sixteenth)	♪, ♫ (sixteenth)
2, 2 2 (eighth)	♪, ♫ (eighth)
2 (quarter)	♩ (quarter)
2. (dotted quarter)	♩. (dotted quarter)
2 (half)	𝅗𝅥 (half)
2 (whole)	𝅝 (whole)

REST VALUES

Tab and Standard Music		
sixteenth note(s)	—	sixteenth rest
eighth note(s)	—	eighth rest
quarter note	—	quarter rest
dotted quarter note	—	dotted quarter rest (𝄽· or 𝄽 𝄾)
half note	—	half rest
whole note	—	whole rest

easy to learn, and keep the standard music notation technically accurate and consistent.

The main difference between the tab and music systems in this book is that music notation represents pitch, while tab specifies what notes are to be played. This is because the six horizontal lines used for tab are a visual representation of the six strings of the guitar, and the numbers specify the fret and string that are played. Standard music notation, however, places notes on a *staff* of five lines (and four spaces) that indicate the more abstract idea of pitch. Because tab is more concrete—essentially a map of the guitar neck—it does not employ leger lines: short horizontal lines used for extending the range of pitches that may be written on a regular staff.

The following shows the same measures in tab (below) and music (above):

Note the use of both lines and spaces, as well as leger lines in the music, while tab uses only the six lines. Note also that the system used for denoting rhythm, the grouping of notes (phrasing), and division of upward and downward stems, are all identical. The only major difference is in the way the actual pitches are conveyed on paper.

Two exceptions are made here, in order to make the tab less confusing and easier to learn:

(1) occasionally, a note sustained over a beat and thus followed by a *tie* in *standard music* (⌒) is often shown in the *tab without* a tie, and is instead followed by a rest sign equal in length to the sustain. (See previous example, beginning of second measure.) Even though a rest is used, implying a silence, the correct overall effect is achieved since the note will automatically keep ringing when played up to tempo. The tie appears in the music since it is more accurate for those who can read standard music and want to refer to it.

(2) Since it is impossible to distinguish a half-note (𝅗𝅥) from a quarter-note (♩) in tablature, both rhythmic values will appear identical, as shown below. (See also previous example, end of second measure.)

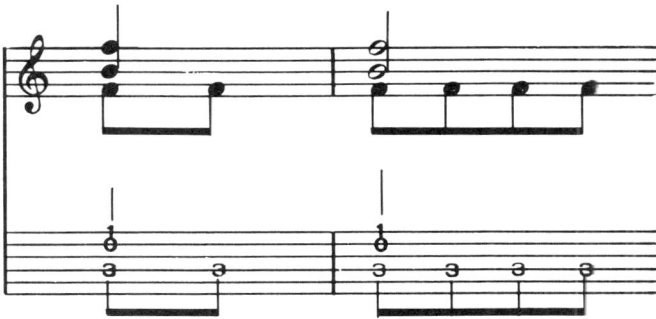

QUARTER NOTES in treble against 8th notes in bass.   HALF NOTES in treble against 8th notes in bass.

Here, the note value is easily clarified by referring to the standard music. Once again, the proper effect is achieved when the phrase is played up to tempo.

In summary, the three major differences between tab and standard music notation are:

(1) The way pitch is shown. Tab uses fret numbers on six lines, while music uses note heads on lines *and* spaces.

(2) Music uses ties as distinct from rests, while tab uses *only* rest signs to represent both effects.

(3) Standard music distinguishes between quarter-notes (♩) and half-notes (𝅗𝅥), while tab does not.

WILLIAM PASKETT

Cordially yours
...mon Jefferson

Blind Lemon Jefferson

Prison Cell Blues

"Yeh, I'll tell you another guy who used to play. I loved to hear him play but couldn't nobody never be lucky enough to dance by his music. That was Lemon Jefferson. He'd break time all the time through his pieces. We saw him play in Grafton and sometimes we'd have little parties or something, you know, when we wasn't playing, 'cause we'd go down to the studios at nine o'clock in the morning and round about twelve we'd come back. Lemon was one of the crack-batters in record-making. He was there recording two days before we got there. He left Friday on his way to Texas. That's when the car wreck was when he got killed."

SON HOUSE

Blind Lemon Jefferson is one of the most interesting guitarists to come out of the South. He recorded many sides during his career but his early pieces show his brilliance at its best. His guitar technique was perhaps the most unique to be recorded. He played tricks with the rhythms that in some cases makes it impossible to tap an even beat. Yet, on hearing all his pieces they never feel choppy or arhythmic.

Some people feel that Lemon used a flatpick and his index and middle finger to play. Others think he used his fingers only. Most likely he used both depending on the song. He recorded an excess of blues in C that closely resemble Jimmie Rodgers's most popular discs. In these, it seems that a flatpick was used while "Black Horse Blues" was obviously finger-picked! There is much similarity between Lemon's "Black Horse Blues" and Rev. Gary Davis's tunes in C. "Easy Rider Blues" is somewhat similar to John Hurt's style, yet it incorporates a counterpoint section that makes it quite different. His blues in E are hard to follow rhythmically for the guitar parts weave in and out of the vocal phrasing. His most important guitar arrangement is "Rabbit Foot Blues." This is played in an open tuning but has a flavor that only Lemon could produce. This boogie-woogie guitar playing was later imitated by many guitarists.

Stephen Calt, who has studied Lemon's lyrics, has mentioned the following points:

1. He was among the most verbally sophisticated, prolific, and emulated of blues songwriters.

2. Many of his verses are nevertheless enigmatic or subtle, so much so that they cannot even be classified as serious, nonsensical or deliberately facetious.

3. His compositions fall into two general categories, both of which are represented by the pieces picked for this book. Between 1926 and mid 1927 he followed the standard operating procedure of country bluesmen by presenting couplets with only internal coherence and only minimal thematic relationships to each other within a given song.

Lemon rarely used a bottleneck and this sound is found only once in his recorded works. From a guitarist's viewpoint he was incredibly versatile. He took a form of blues, be it in the key of C or open C, and presented variations so that each song had a different flavor to it.

It is very important to hear Blind Lemon Jefferson on record and fortunately there are several outstanding reissues of his work. His vocal effects with tone and phrasing are worth studying by themselves.

We open this volume with two of Lemon's easier pieces. In the latter section of the book there are three of his harder and more unusual pieces.

This is a comparatively easy guitar accompaniment and a good piece to begin our study with. Most of the pieces to follow will have no easy rules. Within one song he often combined a variety of techniques. The alternating bass that we associate with Mississippi John Hurt is used in these pieces as well as sections where only treble melody is played. A new technique of double-timing the bass notes will be used in many of the pieces to follow. This is a way to imitate the Ragtime piano styles that were popular during this period.

"Prison Cell Blues" is very similar to Lemon's classic arrangement of "See That My Grave Is Kept Clean." Both pieces are played in regular tuning in the key of E.

You should have no problem in mastering this song. You can hear the original on two excellent reissues (see Discography).

Prison Cell Blues

Gettin' tired of sleepin' in this low-
  down lonesome cell.
Lord, I wouldn't a-been here if it
  hadn't a-been for Nell.

Lay awake at night and just can't
  eat a bite.
Used to be my rider but you just
  won't treat me right.

Got a red-eyed captain, and a
  squabblin' bo.*
Got a mad-dog sergeant, honey,
  and he won't knock off.**

I'm gettin' tired of sleepin' in this
  low-down lonesome cell.
Lord, I wouldn't a-been here if
  it hadn't a-been for Nell.

I asked the government to knock
  some days off my time.
For the way I'm treated, I'm
  'bout to lose my mind.

I wrote to the governor to please
  turn me a-loose.
Since I didn't get no answer, I
  know it t'ain't no use.

I'm gettin' tired of sleepin' in this
  low-down lonesome cell.
Lord, I wouldn't a-been here if it
  hadn't a-been for Nell.

I hate to turn over and find my rider
  gone.
Walks across my floor, Lordy how I
  moan.

Well, I wouldn't a-been here if it
  hadn't a-been for Nell.
I'm gettin' tired of sleepin' in this
  low-down and lonesome cell.

*i.e. mate. "Bo" could also be an
apocopated form of boss.
**Knock off often means to quit
work for the day or stop for a rest.

Easy Rider Blues

This is one of Lemon's most melodic guitar pieces. It begins with an ordinary alternating bass and then introduces a beautiful counterpoint run. This run is repeated several times throughout the arrangement.

It is played in regular tuning in the key of G. It reminds me in parts of John Hurt's "Shake That Thing," yet it introduces a more complex idea in that the melody is sometimes played and other times only hinted at.

We will look at other songs by Blind Lemon further on in this volume. These will be his "weirder" tunes which are played with more rhythmic patterns.

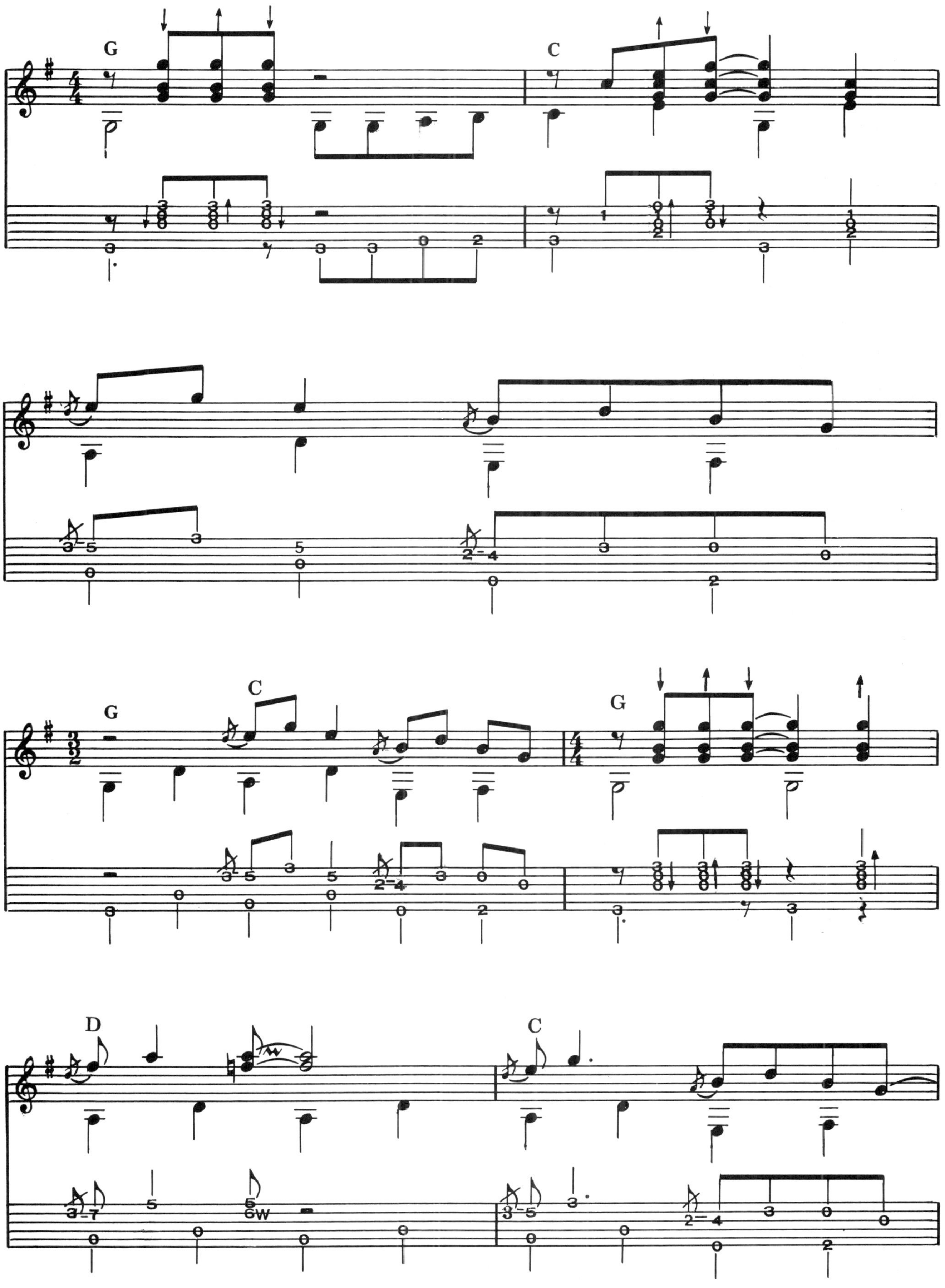
G
C
G
C
G
D
C

Aw, tell me where my easy rider's
  gone.
Tell me where my easy rider's gone.
Well, (anywhere these) women
  always in the wrong.

Your easy rider died on the road.
Man, the easy rider died on the road.
I'm a poor boy here and ain't got
  nowhere to go.

There's gonna be the time that a
  woman don't need no man.
Well, it's gonna be a time (that) a
  woman don't need no man.
Say, baby, shut your mouth and
  don't be raisin' sand.

Train I ride don't burn no coal at all.
Train I ride don't burn no coal at all.
The coal I burn everybody say is the
  cannonball.

I went to the depot,
I mean I went to the depot, sat my
  suitcase down.
The blues overtake me and the tears
  come rollin' down.

Woman I love, she must be out of
  town.
Woman I love, man, she's outta town.
She left me this mornin' with her
  face in a terrible frown.

I got a gal across town, she crochets
  all the time.
I got a gal across town, crochetin' all
  the time.
Sugar, you don't quit crochetin',
  you're gonna lose your mind.

Say fair brown, what's the matter
  now?
Say fair brown, what's the matter
  now?
You're tryin' your best to quit me,
  woman, and you don't know how.

William Moore

One Way Gal

William Moore recorded the following song twice during the twenties. The first recording was an instrumental called "Old Country Rock" which was a take off on Blind Blake's very popular "West Coast Blues." For the second recording, he added lyrics and retitled it "One Way Gal."

There are few tricks to this piece. It is played in ordinary tuning in the key of D. The bass alternates throughout the whole piece with the exception of the end tag when an E7 and A chord are played. Then the right hand breaks up the pattern by putting more syncopation into the bass.

The second guitar break has been transcribed.

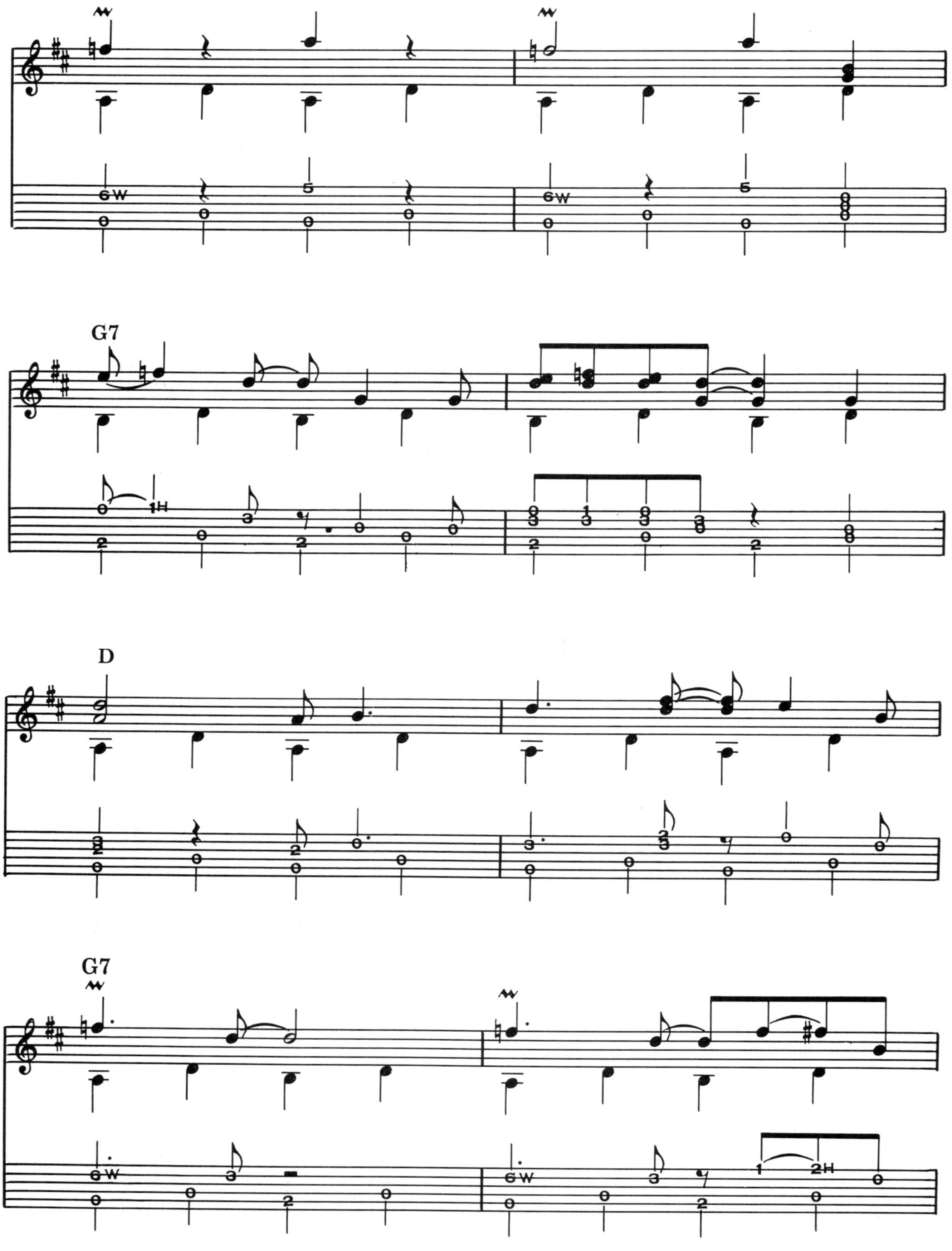
G7
D
G7

D

E7   A

There's one thing I like about that
   gal of mine,
There's one thing I like about that
   gal of mine,
There's one thing I like about that
   gal of mine,
She treats me right and loves me all
   the time.

Sometimes I'm broke and blue as I
   can be,
   (Repeat line twice)
But still my baby, she looks after me.

She walked in the rain till her feet
   got soakin' wet,
   (Repeat line twice)
And these were the words she said to
   ever' man she met:

"Mister change a dollar, give me a
   lousy dime,
   (Repeat line twice)
"So I can feed this hungry man of
   mine."

She took me over to a cabaret,
   (Repeat line twice)
I eat and drink and then I went
   away.

Gal of mine she's one way all the
   time,
   (Repeat line twice)
She takes the blues away and satis-
   fies my mind.

Blind Willie McTell
Stole Rider Blues

"Stole Rider Blues" was transcribed from the playing of Blind Willie McTell—another master of the twelve-string guitar. This tune is almost identical to his great "Statesboro Blues." You will notice that there are positions used in this piece that were also used in Lemon's "Easy Rider Blues." Yet, this tune is in the key of D and "Easy Rider Blues" was in the key of G.

This is a very slow blues. When the verse is being sung the guitar vamps. The guitar plays its licks between the lines. This is a very popular and ordinary way of accompanying blues singing.

Yazoo Records has a wonderful LP completely devoted to Blind Willie McTell that I am sure you will enjoy. The guitar introduction as well as the accompaniment behind the first verse have been transcribed here.

Introduction D

First Verse

I'm goin' grab me a train, ride the
   lonesome rail.
I'm goin' grab me a train, ride the
   lonesome rail.
Nigger stole my baby, she's in the
   lonesome jail.

Hitch up my mama, carried her to
   the Turner Road.
   (Repeat line)
Now she's screamin' and cryin',
   "Father, let your mama come back
   home."

I stole my good gal from my bosom
   friend.
   (Repeat line)
That fool got lucky, he stole her
   back again.

Now the woman I love got a mouth
   chock full of good gold.
   (Repeat line)
Everytime she hug and kiss me it
   makes my blood run cold.

When you see two women runnin'
   hand in hand,
   (Repeat line)
Bet you my last dollar, one done
   stole the other's man.

I'm leavin' town, please don't spread
   the news.
   (Repeat line)
That's why I got these ol' stole rider
   blues.

Rev. Gary Davis

All My Friends Are Gone

Both Rev. Gary Davis and Blind Willie McTell have contributed extensively to the following song.

The arrangement presented here is one that has gone through the mythical experience called "the folk process." I first heard Blind Willie McTell do a song called "Delia." This was a version of "Delia, One More Round" played in a Memphis style. I then mentioned this piece to Rev. Davis and he played another version but had forgotten the words. Weeks later I discovered an old book of words to songs from the Durham, North Carolina area, and sure enough, Rev. Davis's version was in it. I then rearranged the guitar part adding a small counterpoint section.

What follows is a very beautiful accompaniment to a wonderful story. The story is yet another variant of Frankie and Johnny. The guitar playing is quite similar to Rev. Davis's "Cocaine Blues" which has been played by almost every white singer involved in the blues revival. Both Rev. Davis's words to "All My Friends Are Gone" and McTell's "Delia" can be sung to this arrangement.

The bass alternates throughout the piece with the exception of the short counterpoint section. However, the sound you get is quite different from the John Hurt sound. This piece is played in regular tuning in the key of C. Most pieces in the key of C use a bass pattern alternating between the fourth and fifth strings. However, in this song the bass alternates between the fourth and sixth strings. The result is a very different texture. This is a technique that Rev. Davis seems to have developed.

If you are a fan of Rev. Davis's guitar playing, you will hear in this piece several of his trademark sounds. When you play the lick on F, or the opening C lick, you should be reminded of many of his arrangements. Rev. Davis is incredible in that he has mastered many different styles.

All My Friends Are Gone

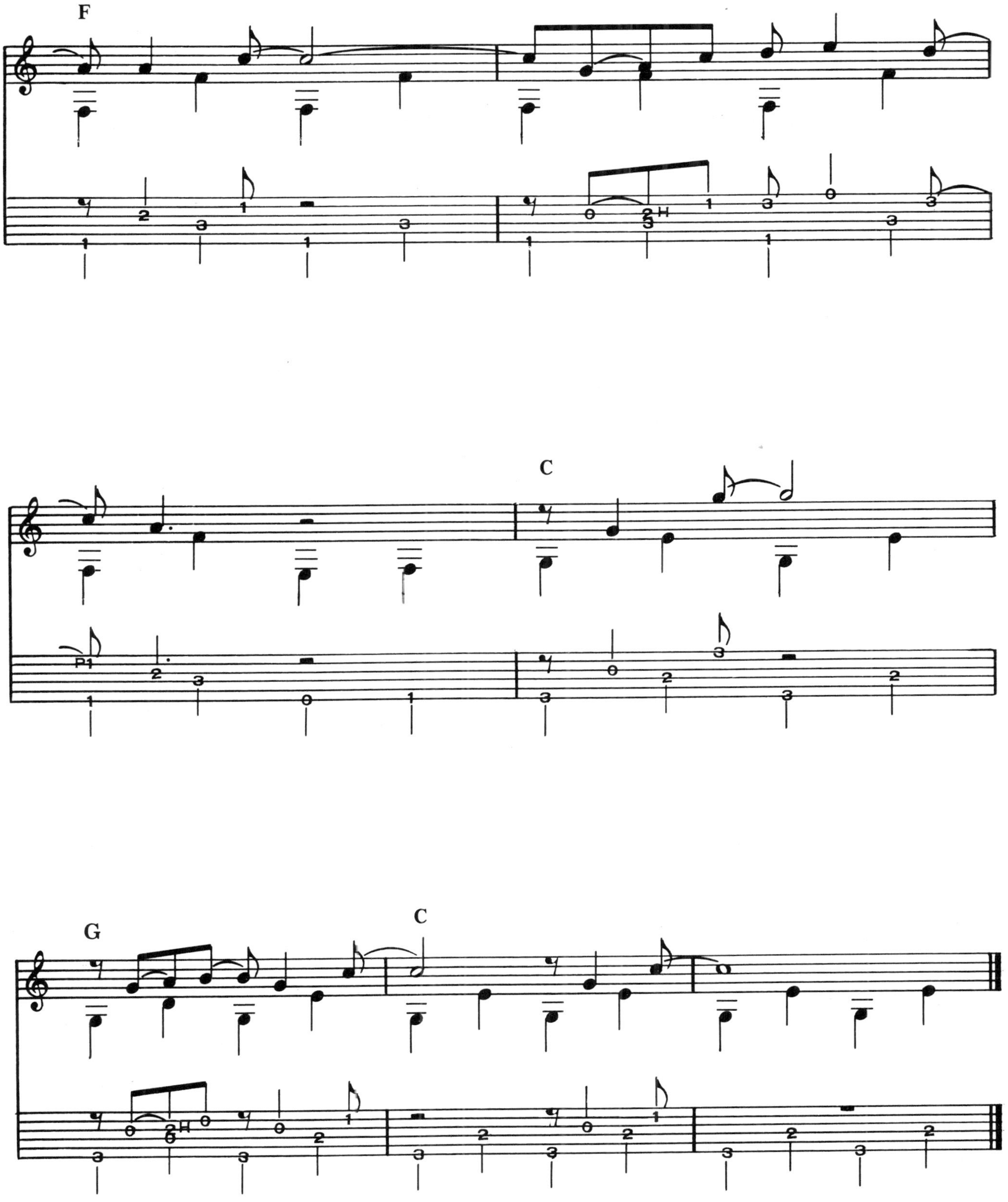
F
C
G
C

First Version:
"All My Friends Are Gone"
Rev. Gary Davis

*Delia, Delia was a-goin' her last
  go round
When ol' coon came by
And shot her to the ground.
All the friends I had are gone.*

*Delia, Delia made a lunge to run,
Sheriff shot her down
With his great big Gatlin' gun.
All the friends I ever had are gone.*

*Rubber-tired carriage, rubber-tired
  hack
Done took poor Delia to the bone
  yard,
Ain't never brought her back.
All the friends I ever had are gone.*

*Men in Atlanta tryin' to pass fo'
  white.
Delia's in the graveyard
Six feet out of sight.
All the friends I ever had are gone.*

*Men in Atlanta drinkin' out a silver
  cup
Delia's in the graveyard,
Ain't never goin' to get up.
All the friends I ever had are gone.*

*Delia, Delia, how could it be?
Wanted everyone,
But you never had time for me.
All the friends I ever had are gone.*

Second Version:

"Delia"
Blind Willie McTell

*Delia was a gambler, gambled all
  around.
She was a gamblin' girl,
She's layin' her money down.
She's all I got is gone.*

*Delia see her mother, took a trip out
  West.
When she returned,
Little Delia had gone to rest.
She's all I got is gone.*

*Delia's Mother weeped, Delia's
  father moaned.
Wouldn't hurt so bad,
But chile died at home.
She's all I got is gone.*

*Delia, Delia, how can it be?
Say you love them rounders
And don't love me.
She's all I got is gone.*

*Cutty's he's in the barroom, drinkin'
  out of a silver cup.
Delia she's in the graveyard
May not never wake up.
She's all I got is gone.*

*Rubber-tired buggy, double-seated
  hack,
Taken Delia to the cemetery
But failed to bring her back.
She's all I got is gone.*

*Delia, Delia poor girl she's gone.
All I have
She has left me all alone.
She's all I got is gone.*

*Judge said to Cutty, "What that
  fuss about?"
"All account of those gamblers
Tryin' to drive me out."
She's all I got is gone.*

*Cutty said to the judge, "What
  might be my fine?"
"I done told you poor boy
You got ninety-nine."
She's all I got is gone.*

*Up on the house top, high as I
  can see,
Lookin' at those rounders
Lookin' after me.
She's all I got is gone.*

*Curly lookin' high, curly lookin' low,
Shot poor Delia down
With that April 44.
She's all I got is gone.*

Blind Boy Fuller

Little Woman, You're So Sweet

Blind Boy Fuller was the most popular bluesman to come out of the Carolinas. He learned much of his technique from the great Rev. Gary Davis who lived in Durham. Davis recalls that before Fuller came to him he was playing only "knife guitar." In Fuller's large recorded works there is only one or two knife pieces found.

His guitar style is not an imitation of Davis's. It is much simpler and perhaps easier to like on first listening. It is a perfect accompaniment to his voice which had a superb quality for blues and rags. He varied his recorded works from hard blues to minstrel show songs, rags, Ragtime songs and gospel pieces. On many of his discs he is accompanied by Sonny Terry on harmonica and Bull City Red on washboard. This sound became a trademark that was widely imitated among blacks as well as white revivalists. Brownie McGhee along with Sonny Terry carry this tradition on to this day. In fact, they still do many of Fuller's original numbers.

The record company used Blind Boy Fuller to compete with Big Bill Broonzy. When Broonzy came out with a particular type of number, it was covered by Fuller for his area. This did not last a long time, for when Broonzy added pianos and horns Fuller continued to use only guitar and harmonica.

His guitar technique uses a fingerpicking style that is easy to master. The distinct sound that you hear on his 78s is gotten by using a steel-bodied National guitar. This sound is produced through a cone-shaped resonator placed in the guitar. This type of instrument was very popular among bluesmen because of its low cost and long life. Before this became popular, the Stella guitar was widely used. The National had another advantage in that it was extremely loud, and since most of the bluesmen sung on the streets or in noisy clubs this was very important.

We have picked a good cross-section of Fuller's work. We have blues in regular tuning and in open tuning. We also included two types of Ragtime pieces. There are many other songs that would probably interest you and I strongly suggest you hear the Blues Classics reissue of Blind Boy Fuller.

This is our first Blind Boy Fuller piece. It is a blues played in open-D tuning (D A D F♯ A D).

Many of Fuller's tunes are similar to Blind Blake's, except that Blake's arrangements are much more complex in fingering and rhythmic ideas. "Police Dog Blues" (page 97), played in open-E tuning, is much more intricate and Ragtime sounding than the more "low down" "Little Woman, You're So Sweet."

You won't encounter anything too difficult in this piece, but you should try to hear the original. No alternating bass is used at all, making this piece sound rather like a field holler put to music.

The guitar part behind the fourth verse has been transcribed.

Little Woman, You're So Sweet

Hey, mama, hey gal.
Don't you hear me callin' you?
You're so sweet, so sweet, my baby,
  so sweet.

Said I love my baby, love her to her
I hate to see my sweet sugar go home.
She's so sweet, so sweet, my little
  woman, so sweet.

See my baby comin', don't get so
  smart.
I'll cut your little within' her and I
  will hug your heart.
You're so sweet, so sweet, my little
  baby, so sweet.

Hey, mama, yea, gal.
Don't you hear Blind Boy Fuller
  callin' you?
She's so sweet, yea sweet, my little
  woman, so sweet.

Hey, mama, yea, gal.
Don't you hear me callin' you?
She's so sweet, so sweet, my little
  woman, so sweet.

Woman I love, she done gone back
  home.
When I think I'm treatin' her right
  I must be doing wrong.
She's so sweet, so sweet, my little
  woman, so sweet.

I'll make a million trips, where I
  would rather be.
But the woman I love is sweeter
  than anything in this world to me.
She's so sweet, so sweet, my little
  woman, sho sweet.

Hey, mama, yea, gal.
Don't you hear Blind Boy Fuller
  callin' you?
You're so sweet, hey sweet, my
  little woman, so sweet.

You've Got Something There

This is a typical Ragtime song of the twenties and thirties. It was so popular that Blind Boy Fuller recorded the music over two dozen times putting different words to each record. Big Bill Broonzy and Blind Blake recorded this melody as well.

Big Bill's "Shuffle Rag" is quite similar to this tune. Only the first guitar break has been transcribed here. It combines an alternating bass with a treble run. This run occurs in the first four measures, and defines the whole mood of the piece. It is played in regular tuning in the key of C.

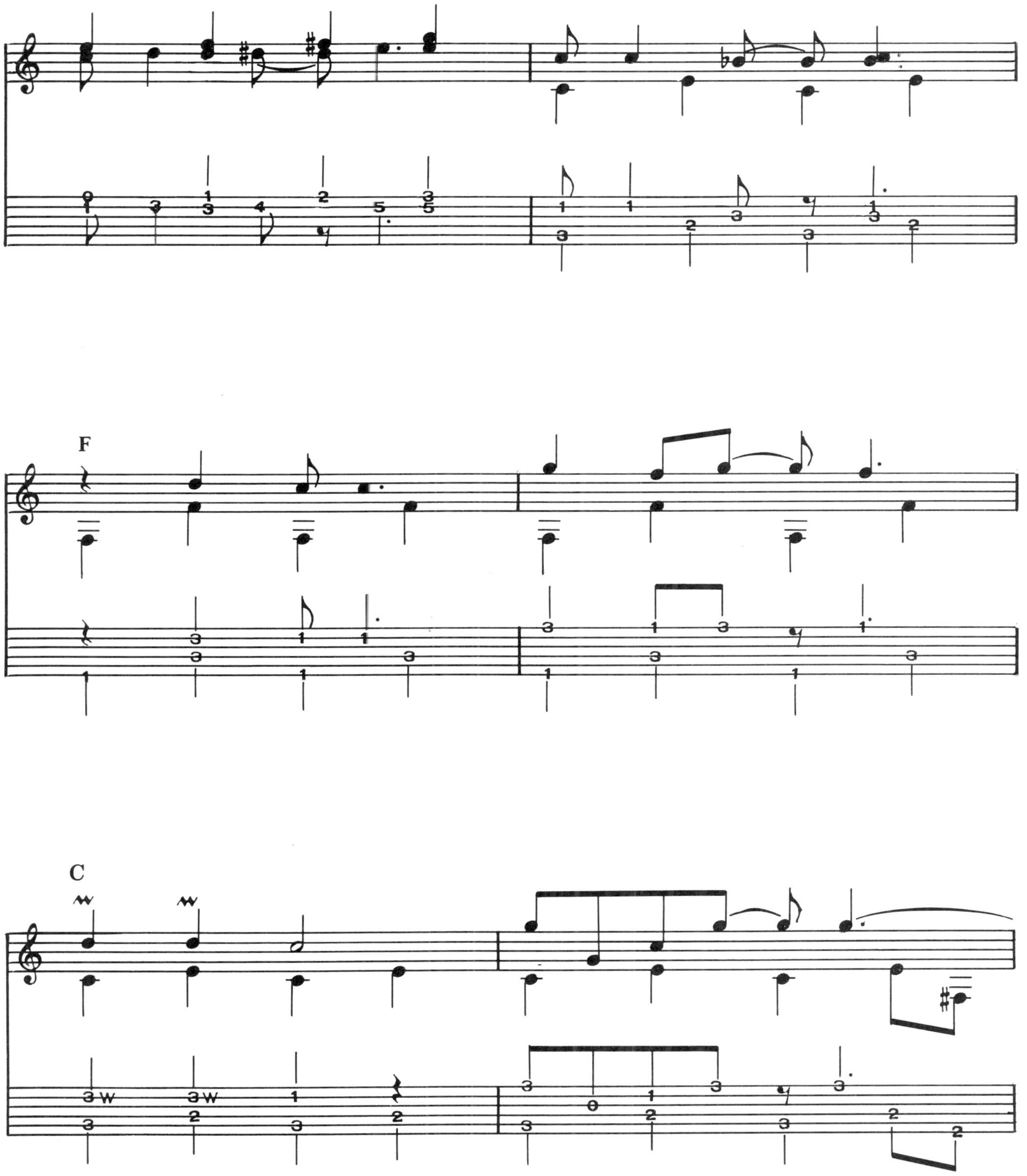
F
C

My gal went uptown 'cause she
  lookin' well.
She fell down, mouth flew open like
  a country well.

Chorus:
She got something there. She got
  something there.
Now I keep on telling you, I know
  she got something there.

Now if you go out, stay all night.
Look here baby, goin' to fuss and
  fight.

Chorus:
You got something there. You got
  something there.
Now I keep on thinkin' 'bout, I
  know you got something there.

She's still just little and I say round.
She can look good as long as you
  can look down.

Chorus:
You got something there. You got
  something there.
Now don't you hear me tellin' you,
  I know she got something there.

Get out now boys, let me shut your
  door.
I got to truck, just before you go.

Chorus:
You got something there. You got
  something there.
Now I keep on telling you, I know
  she got something there.

Gonna tell you boys just because
  you my pals.
It's a mighty bad sign to advertise
  your gal.

Chorus:
You got something there. You got
  something there.
Now don't you hear me singin' 'bout,
  I know she got something there.

Piccolo Rag

Rev. Gary Davis first taught me this piece. It is another tune that has been recorded many times with different words. The most famous version of this tune was recorded by Blind Blake in the twenties. He played it as an instrumental and called it "West Coast Blues" (page 104). Fuller's arrangement is the simplest of the three and uses an alternating bass throughout the piece with the exception of the guitar part behind the verse. Here, a two-finger roll is used which I associate with Rev. Davis's playing. Use your thumb and index finger only in this section, to get the proper accenting.

The tune is played in regular tuning in the key of C. There are many chords used that might be new to you. This is one of the great "party songs."

The first guitar break has been transcribed.

Break   C   A7

D7   G7   C

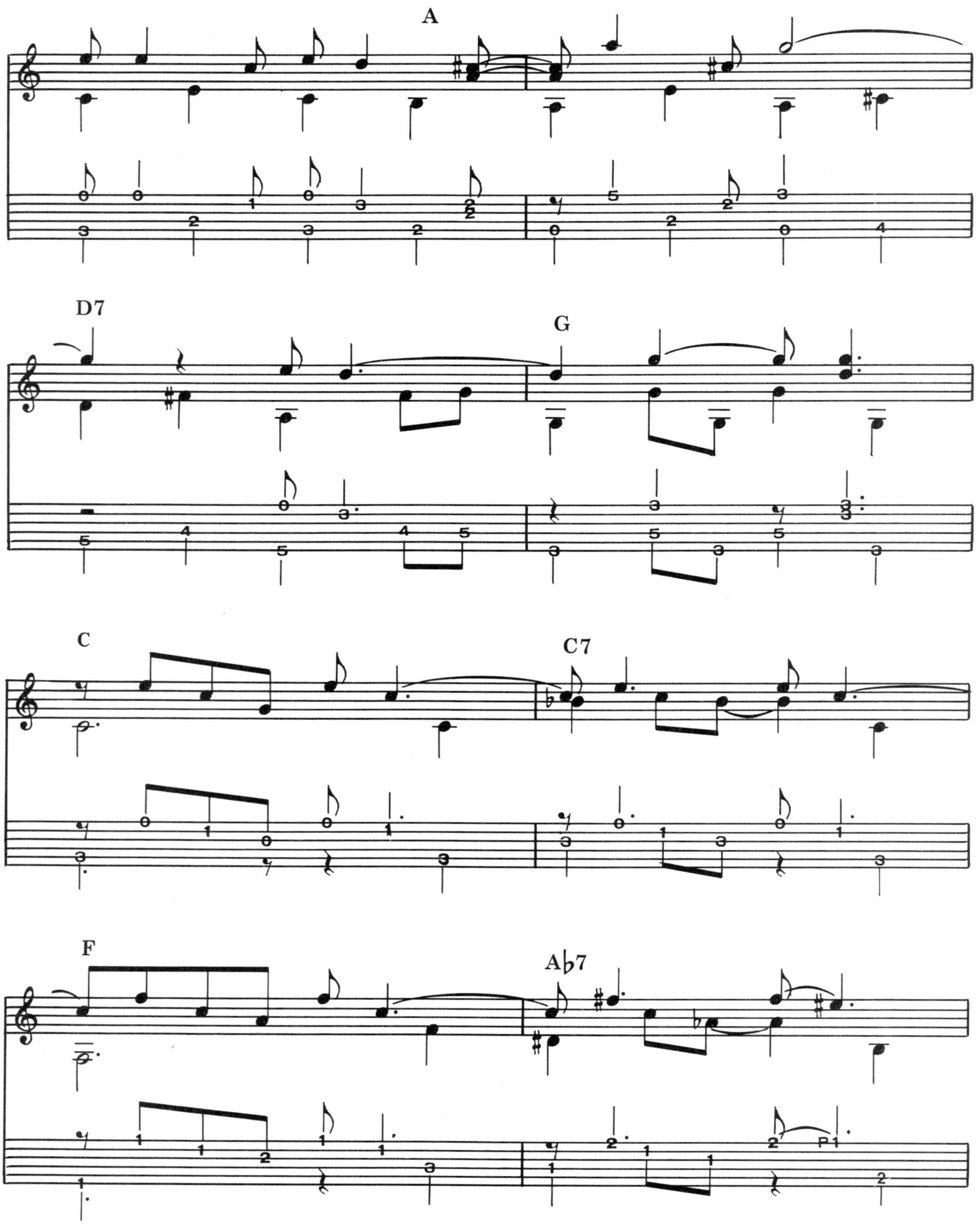
A
D7
G
C
C7
F
A♭7

First Chorus:
*Gotta stop doing what you're doing
  to me, mama,*
You don't, goin' run me wild.
*Gotta stop doing what you're doing
  to me, baby,*
Mean just what I say.

You talk about lovin' that sure is hid,
*You done made me love it and it just
  won't quit.*

Second Chorus:
*Gotta stop doing what you're doing
  to me,*
You don't, goin' run me wild, I mean,
Just gonna run me wild.

*Said when I'm on the corner hollerin'
  "Whoa! Haw! Gee!"*
*My gal's uptown hollerin' "Who
  wants me?"*

*Every night I come home you got
  your lips painted red.*
*Said, "Come on Daddy and let's go
  to bed."*

Got great big legs and little bitty feet.
*Something about you is sweet, sweet,
  sweet*

*You think you're the best lookin' gal
  in town.*
*You do let that love go 'round and
  'round.*

Careless Love

This could be the most popular blues of the last sixty years. It has been recorded by countless artists and is probably known in every house in America. This version is quite different from any other. It is played in a very North Carolina style. A style that Rev. Davis seems to have taught to many of his contemporaries such as Blind Boy Fuller and Brownie McGhee.

The piece is played in regular tuning in the key of A. Fuller used this arrangement several times for other songs. His "Corrina, Corrina" has the same music. Try to listen to Rev. Davis's version of "Twelve Gates to the City," as it has many similar ideas in it.

There is no alternating bass used and again I suggest that you try to hear the original. This is a very distinctive and beautiful way of playing blues in A. This is one of the few "rough" blues that uses a diminished chord effectively.

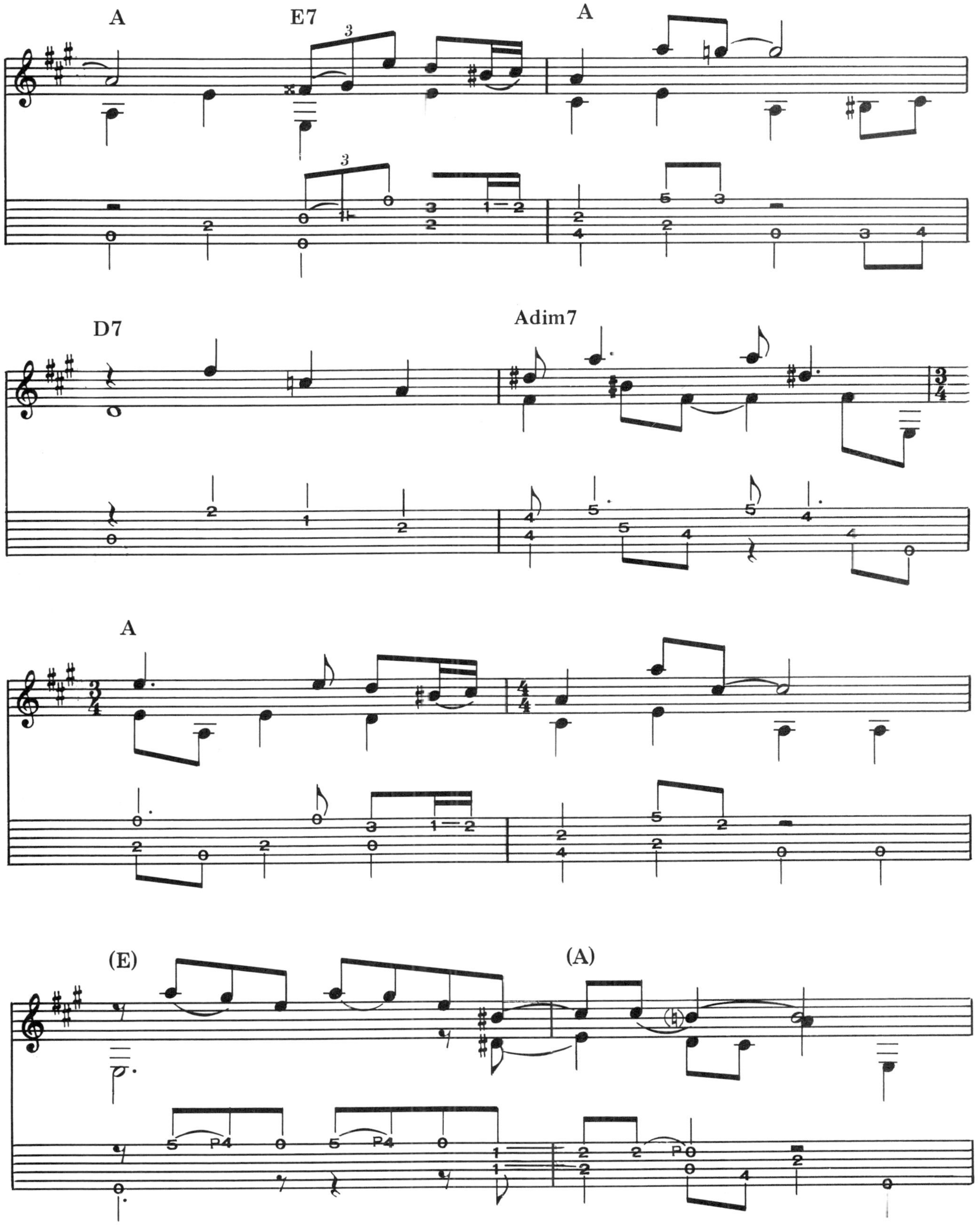
A
E7
A
D7
Adim7
A
(E)
(A)

Oh, love, oh, love, careless love.
Oh, love, love, oh, careless love.
Oh, love, oh, love, oh, careless love.
Don't you see, what careless lovers do?

And it cause' you to leave your used
  to home.
And it cause' you to leave, cause'
  you to moan.
And it cause' you to leave and caused
  you to moan.
And it caused you have to leave your
  happy home.

Now love, oh, love, careless love.
Oh, love, love, oh, careless love.
And it's love, oh, love, I mean, oh,
  careless love.
I want you to see, what careless love
  has done.

Now it's Lord have mercy on poor
  me.
And it's Lord have mercy on poor
  me.
And it's Lord have mercy — mmm —
  poor me.
It's nothin' but troublin' in the world
  I see.

Now all my money you could spend.
Says all my money that you could
  spend.
Now it's all my money that you
  could spend.
Even passed my door and you
  wouldn't look in.

Big Bill Broonzy

Willie Mae

*"Blues is a natural fact, is some-
thing that a fellow lives. If you
don't live it you don't have it...
young people have forgotten to
cry the blues. Now they talk
and get lawyers and things."*

BIG BILL BROONZY

Big Bill Broonzy was perhaps
the most recorded blues artist
to have lived. His career started
as far back as 1927 and continued until his death in 1958.
During this span of time, he
recorded everything from hard
country blues to happy Ragtime numbers to small band
Chicago blues. He is one of the
first bluesmen who was completely accepted by white folk-
revivalists. Most of the young
guitarists I know started by
learning his pieces, whether
folk tunes or blues.

"As popular entertainer,
Broonzy differs significantly
from Broonzy the 'blues am-
bassador' in that his sounds are
predominantly those of the ragtime guitarist. The accelerated
tempos and guitar grandstanding
which made him a hitmaker
among also-rans and formidable
competition like Memphis
Minnie and Blind Boy Fuller

gave way to a slower, more sedate style as Broonzy became folk-oriented. Somewhat ingeniously, he offered the modified style of his twilight years as a throwback, declaring: 'Even the people in the South are learning to play fast time. . . if I was to stop playing the real old slow blues, I don't know what would become of it.' "

Stephen Calt, Nick Perls and Michael Stewart from the album notes to *Young Bill Broonzy* (Yazoo Records, 1011).

Big Bill was born in Mississippi in 1898. He originally played fiddle but put it down to learn guitar. The style that he developed seems unrelated to any other Mississippi player. It is similar in right-hand technique to many guitarists of Texas like Mance Lipscomb or Lightning Hopkins. All keep a steady drone beat in the bass. The bass is also damped, which gives a very unusual effect. This is explored in the selections we have picked to learn. One result from this style is the funny chordal sound that develops. Broonzy once tried to explain this to the more "sophisticated" musicians. "When my song sounds good to me and for me to really sing the old blues that I learned in Mississippi, I have to go back to my sound and not the right chords as the musicians have told me to make."

In his later years, once he had been rediscovered, Broonzy traveled throughout Europe spreading the "news of the blues." His definition of "the blues" is quite interesting.

"Well, frankly I think that the blues is the kind of a thing that you don't have to be without everything to have the blues. . . because I've had as high as two or three hundred dollars in my pocket and was in a place where I couldn't get food and couldn't get nothing to eat. It's true, because I didn't know how to ask for it. I was in a neighborhood that was in France, and the people didn't understand me, and I didn't understand them. So I couldn't tell them what I wanted, and I didn't get it. But the lacking of money. . . I had the money. I just couldn't get what I wanted. That was the main thing. And the same with a lot of people in the South. Lot of people in Mississippi, Texas, Georgia, Alabama, Tennessee, and Kentucky, in those places, they sing the blues and they feel it. But if you go down there they're living a darn sight better than a lot of Negroes in Chicago and New York today. They got their homes. They live the way they want to. They got plenty of food and everything. I bet you they got the money.

"I learnt how to sing and play the blues from my uncle who was a slave. And til today I know from what he's told me that they really suffered. You know, 'cause it wasn't enough for them to halfway live. They had to just live the best they could. So, therefore, that's where the blues actually came from. From those things. People singing about the conditions of life."

This piece has always been a favorite of mine. Like most of Big Bills's songs it has a certain swing to it that makes it unique. Compare this blues in A to "Careless Love." Broonzy used a technique that I associate mainly with Texas guitarists. Instead of a clear alternating bass with two distinct pitches, he damps the lower strings with his right-hand palm. The resulting "thuds" can help make performing simpler because you can continue to accentuate the beat without worrying about fretting accurately. You can play very difficult chords without considering what bass notes are being sounded. If they were to be heard too clearly, the harmony might be too unusual for the average listener's ear. Damping also helps disguise any gross harmonic "violations" that you may have to make just to keep the song moving.

Mance Lipscomb is a great Texas bluesman who uses only this technique. He can be heard on several albums released by Arhoolie Records. This style is explored further in *Texas Blues* (Oak Publications).

This tune is played in regular tuning and can be heard on *Blues* (Folkways Records). There is also a superb reissue of old Big Bill Broonzy recordings available on Yazoo Records.

The first guitar break has been transcribed.

Willie Mae

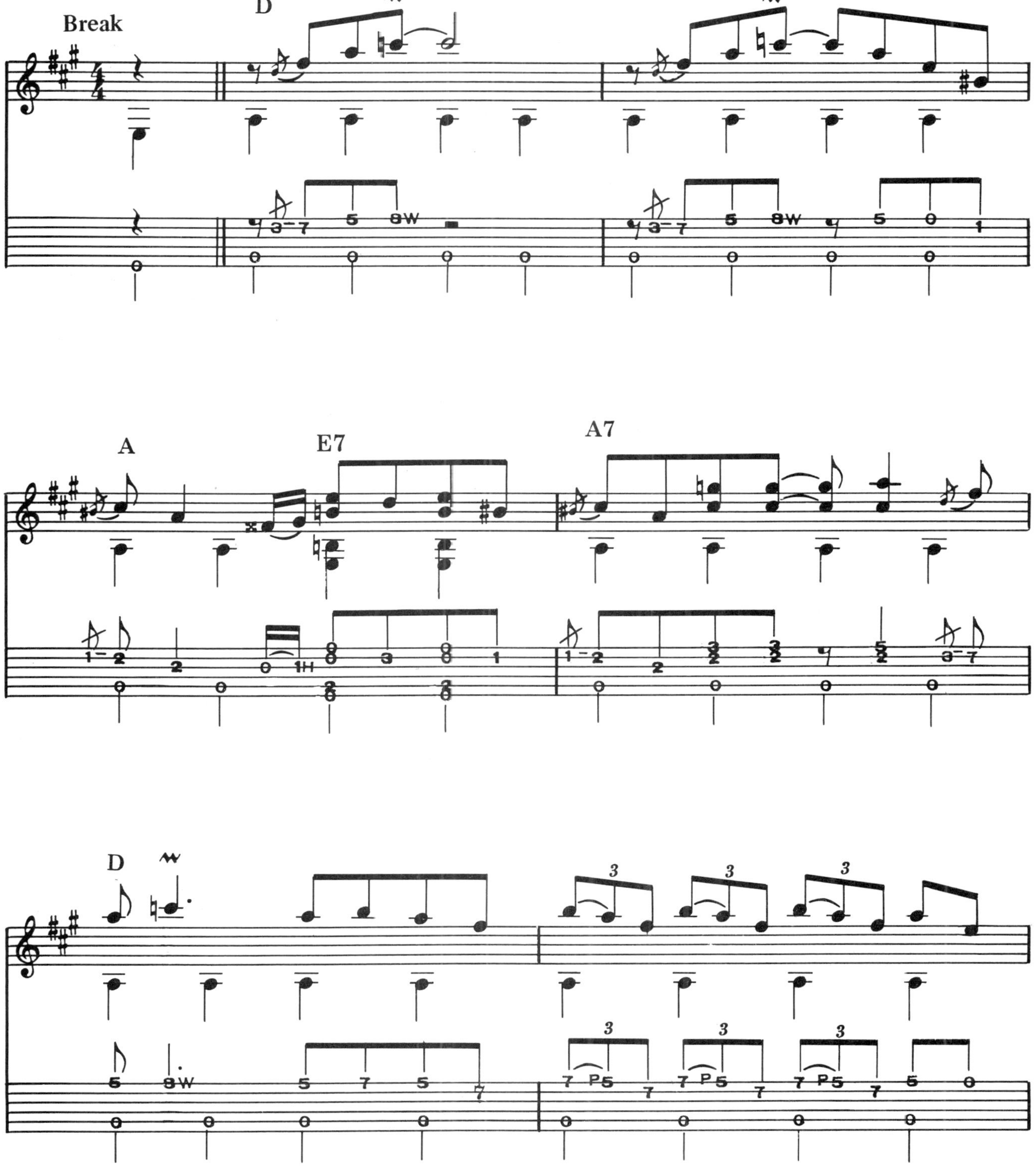

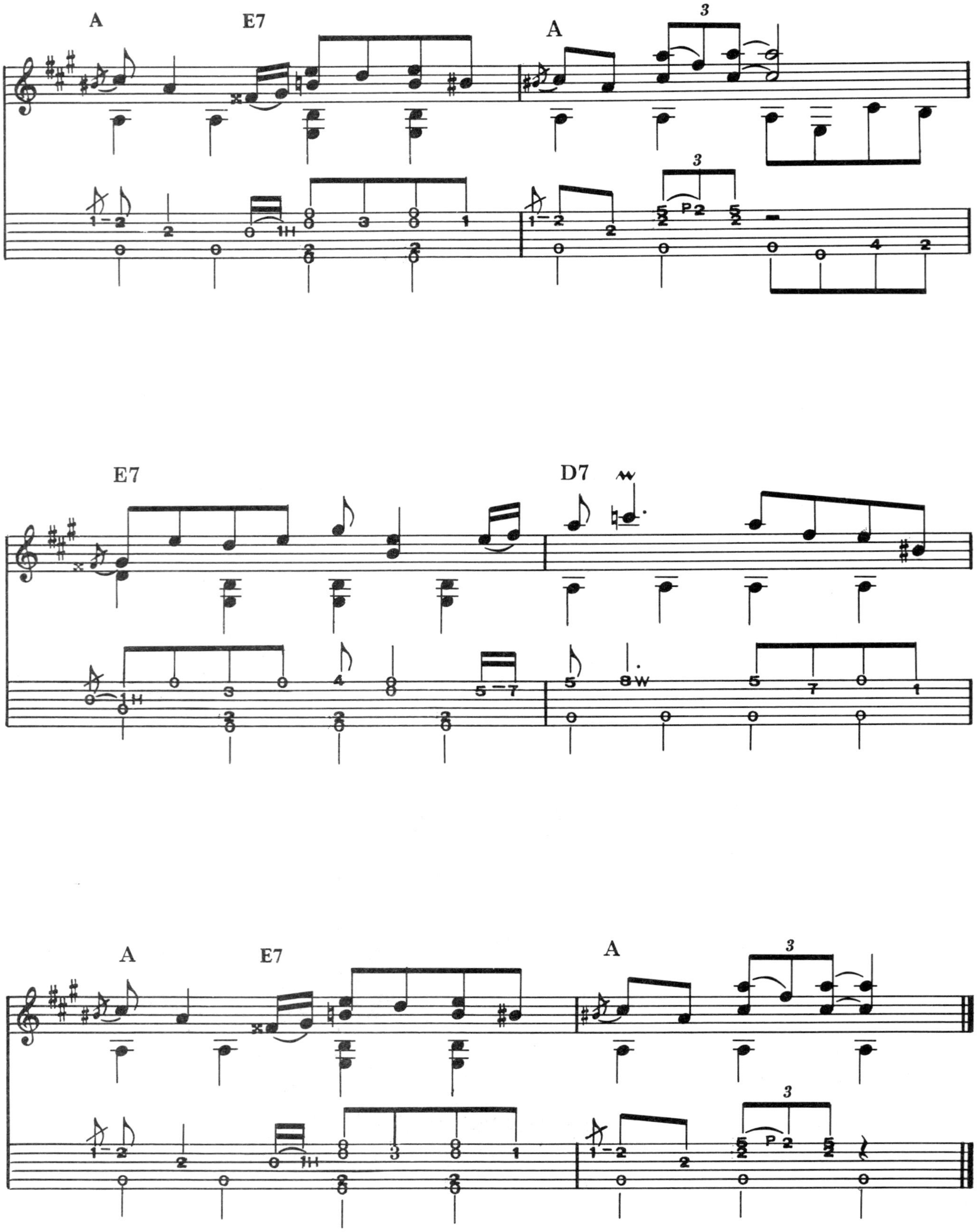
A
E7
A
E7
D7
A
E7
A

*I got a girl named Willie Mae, and
  she lives in the low, low lands.
I got a gal named Willie Mae, and she
  lives in the low, low lands.
Lord, the way I got that woman, I
  declare I stole her from a man.*

*All my life, baby, you know I've
  had to roam.
All my life, Willie Mae, you know
  I've had to roam.
Lord, just on the count of me break-
  ing up one poor man's home.*

*Willie Mae, Willie Mae,
Willie Mae, don't you hear Bill calling
  you?
Lord, if I don't get my Willie Mae,
  there's no other woman will do.*

*When I get to thinking about Willie
  Mae, cold chills creeps up and
  down my spine.
When I get to thinking about Willie
  Mae, cold chills creeps up and
  down my spine.
Sometimes I wish I was dead, Willie
  Mae, you know I'm afraid of dying.*

*I'm going to leave here, baby, and
  I'm going on down the line.
You know I don't do nothing here,
  Willie Mae, but grieving and crying.
You know I don't, don't do nothing
  here, Willie Mae, but grieve and cry.*

Shuffle Rag

This is a wonderful guitar instrumental. It is similar to Blind Boy Fuller's "You've Got Something There." It is played in regular tuning in the key of C. As we have already explained in the previous tune, no alternating bass is used. Remember to damp the bass or you will get a strange result. Listen to the first few measures with damping and without damping.

You should try to hear the original as this will help you to understand the feeling of this piece much better than words can describe.

Three guitar breaks have been transcribed.

Shuffle Rag
Break

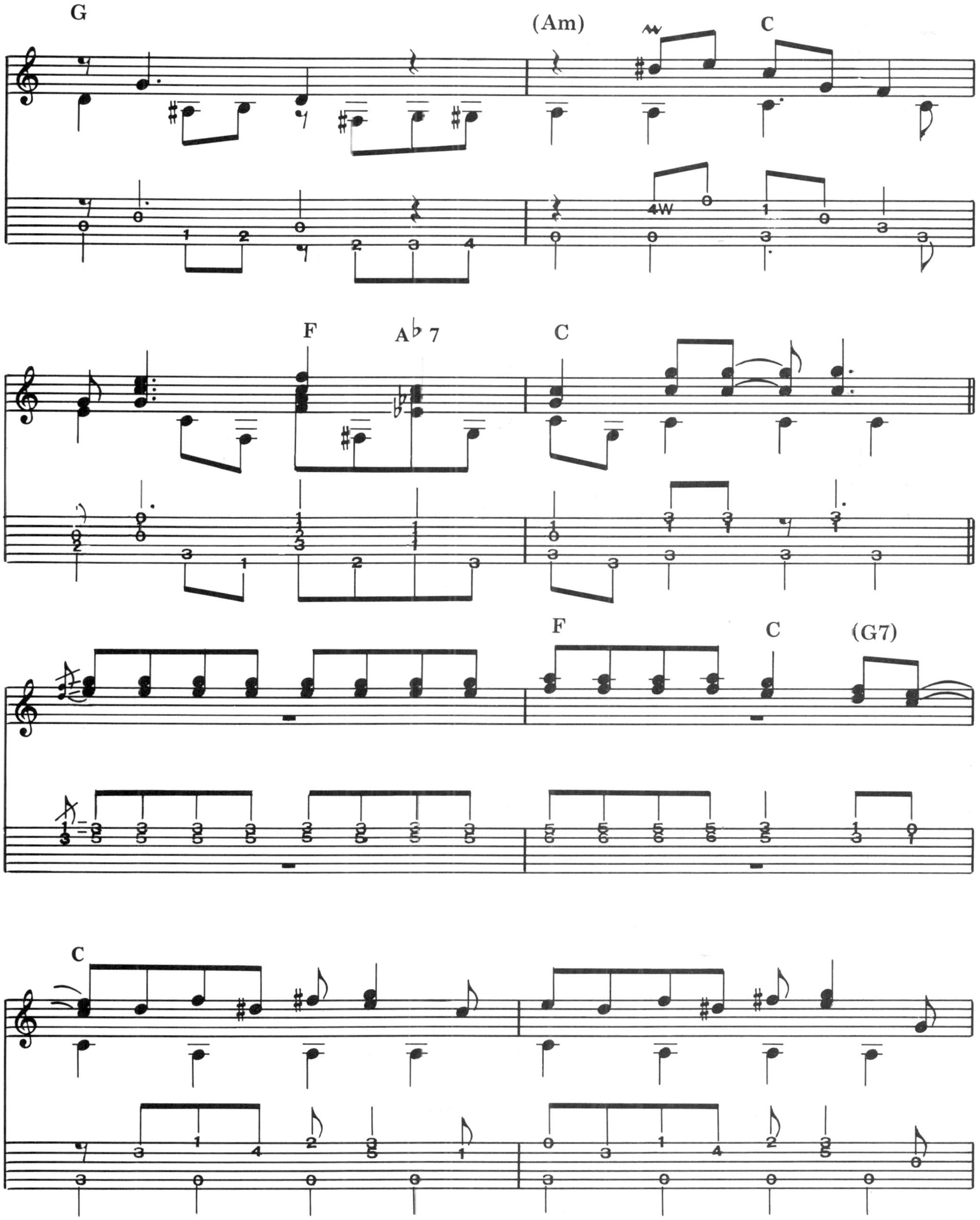
G
(Am)
C
F
A♭ 7
C
F
C
(G7)
C

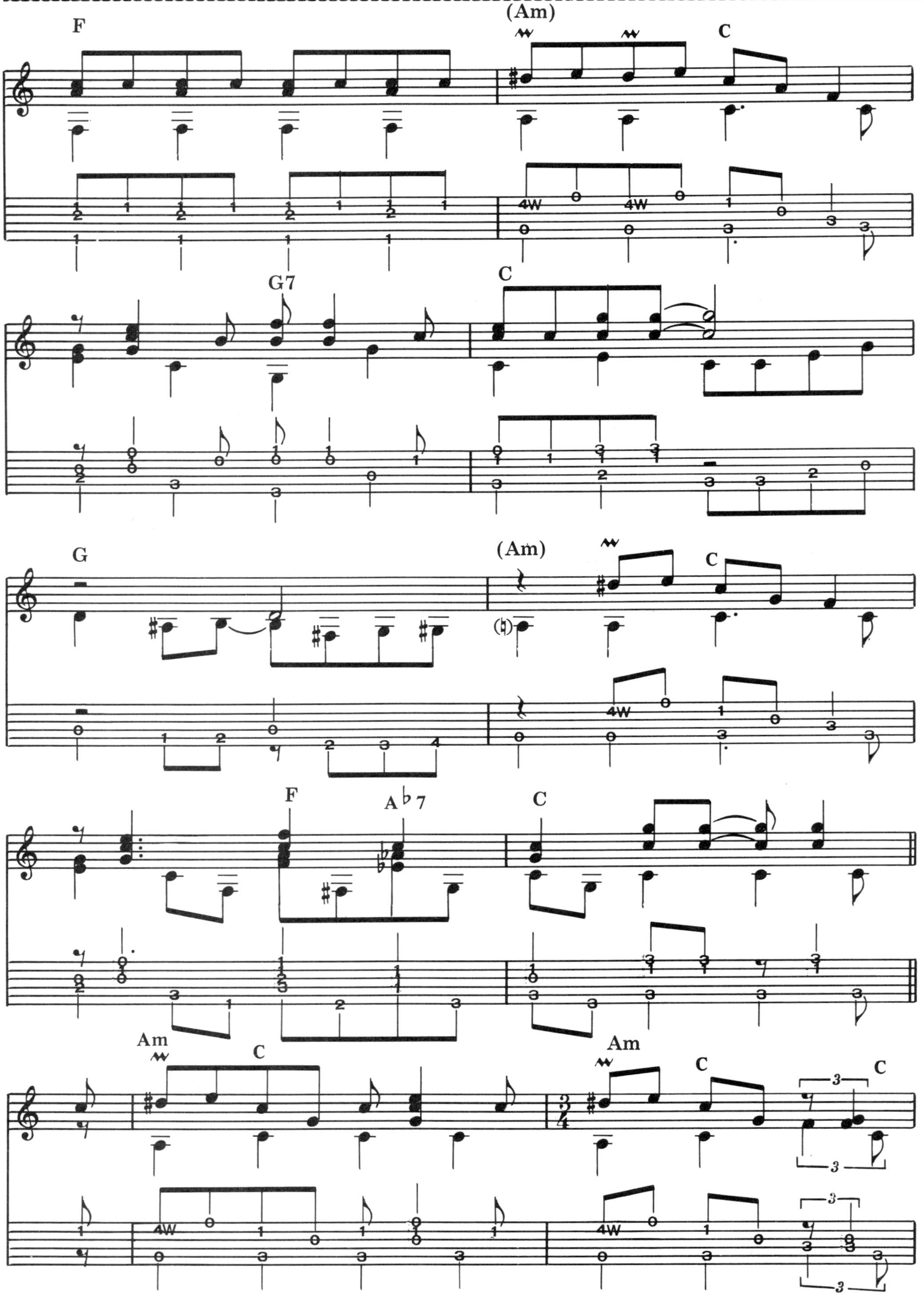
F
(Am)
C
G7
C
G
(Am)
C
F
A♭7
C
Am
C
Am
C
C

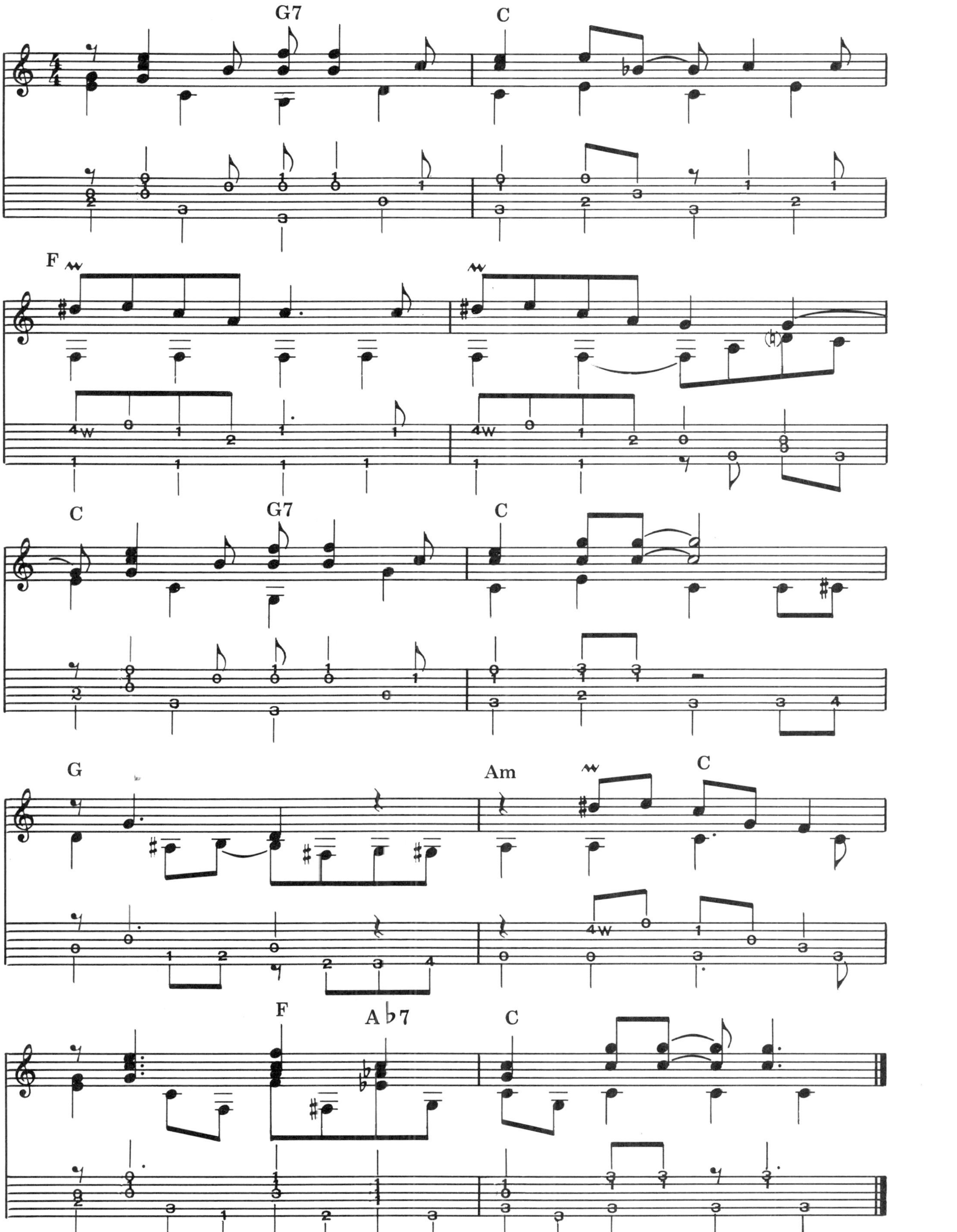
G7
C
F
C
G7
C
G
Am
C
F
A♭7
C

Sam McGee

Franklin Blues

"Franklin Blues" is a rather difficult piece, originally recorded by Sam McGee, the same guitarist who did "Buck Dancer's Choice." It's an instrumental dance tune with three very different sections. There is no alternating bass and the chords change at a rapid pace.

Try to hear the original if possible. It is available on County Records. Arhoolie Records has put together a record of some of Sam McGee's 1969-70 sessions that might be of interest to you.

Franklin Blues

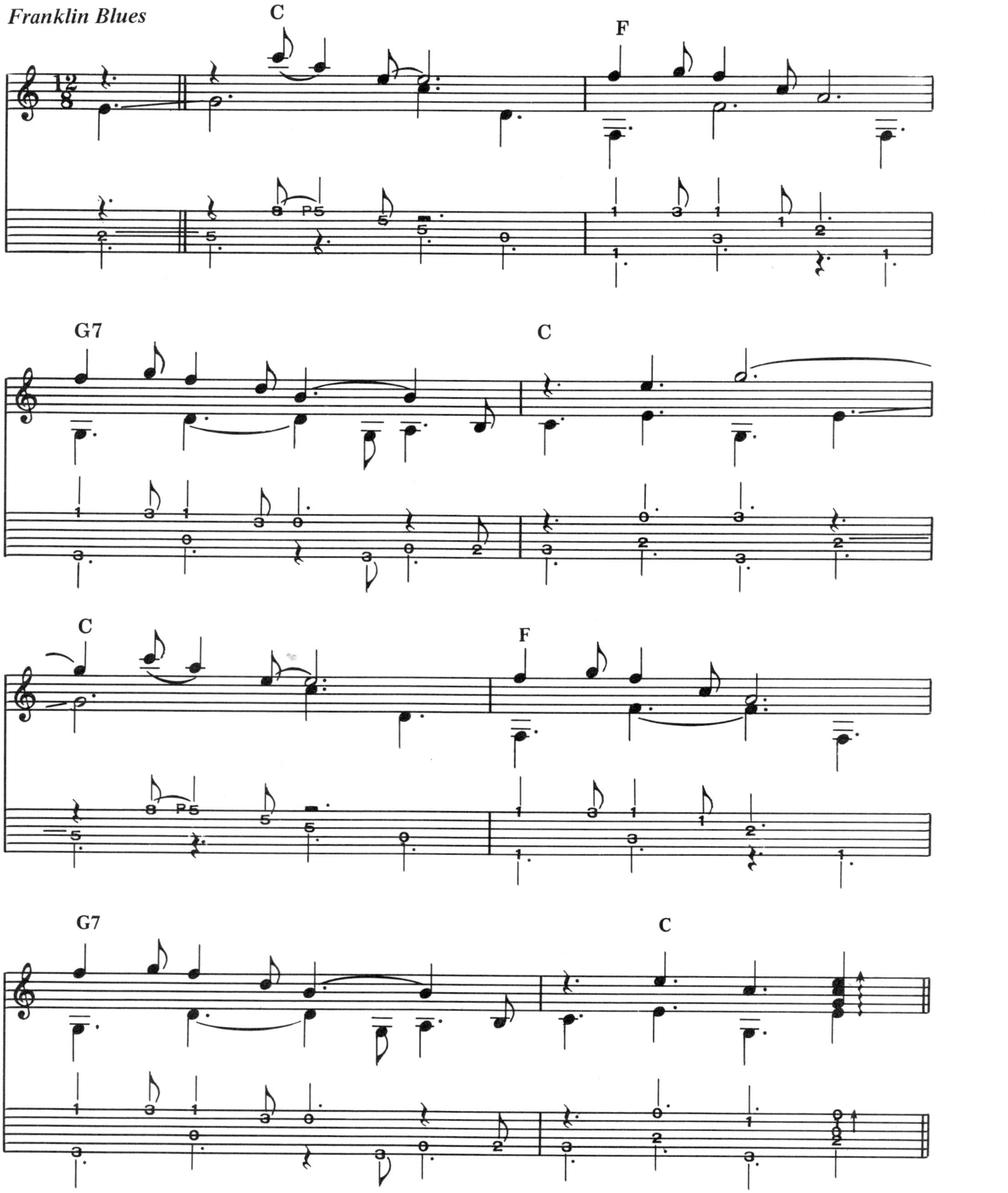

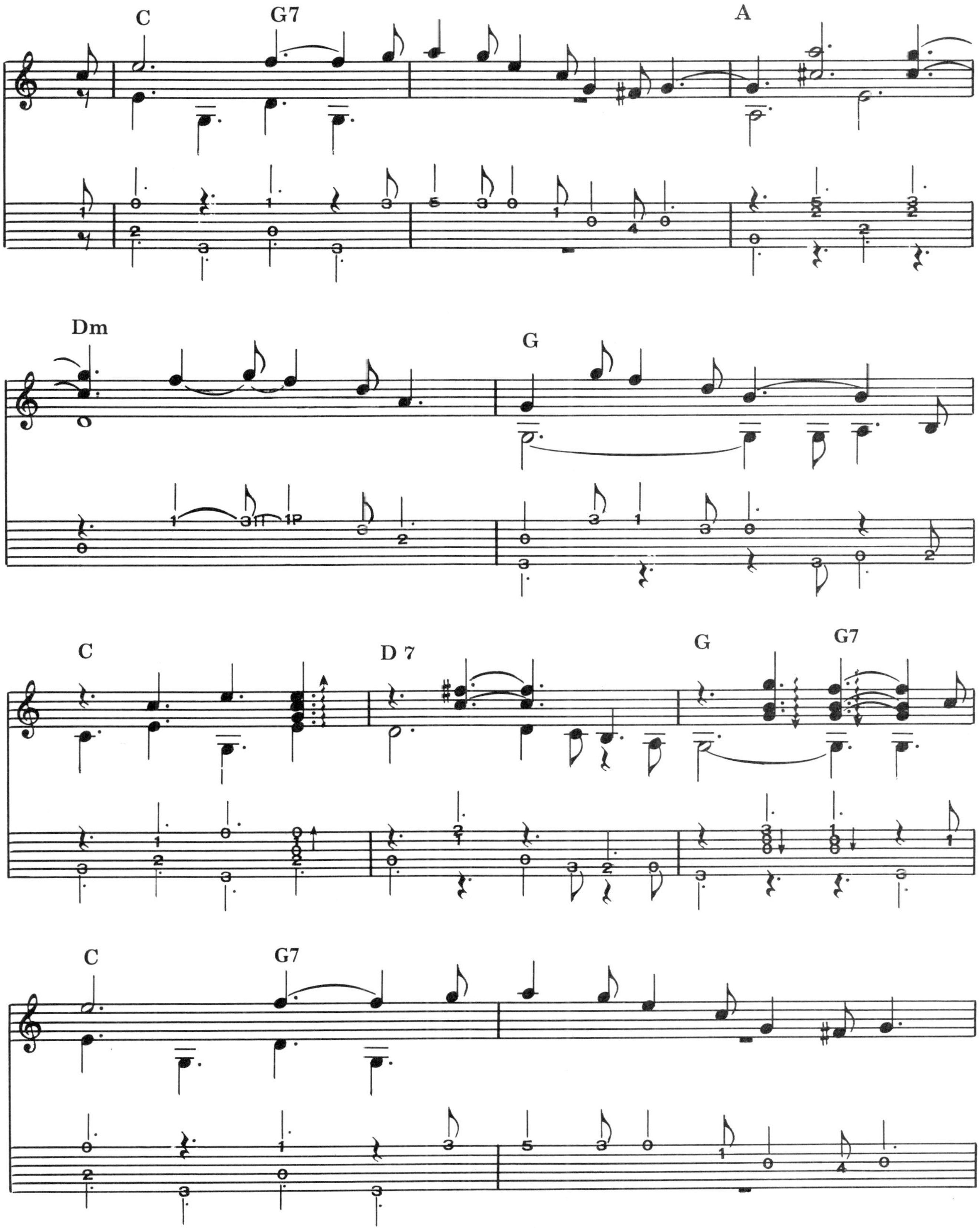
C
G7
A
Dm
G
C
D 7
G
G7
C
G7

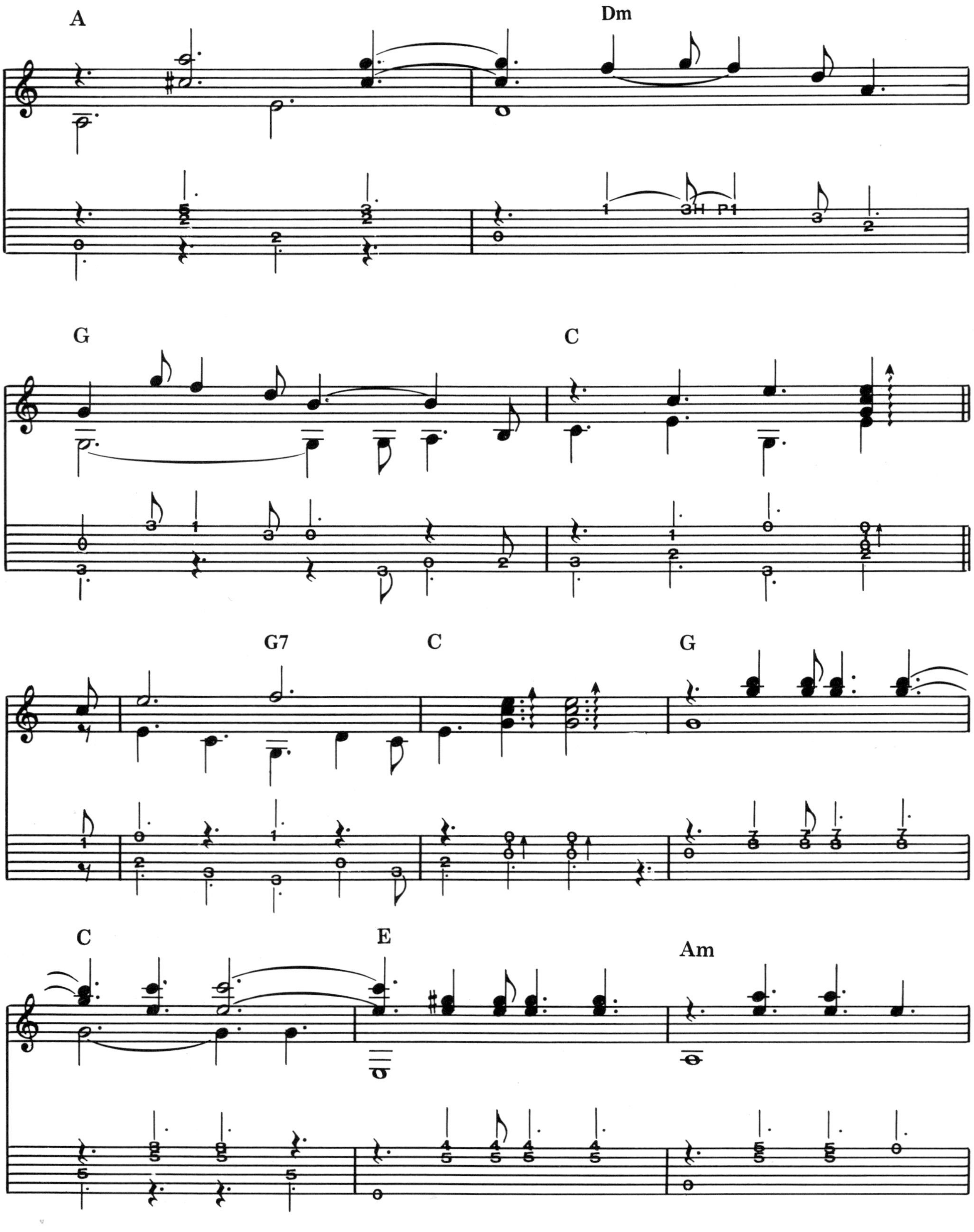
A
Dm
G
C
G7
C
G
C
E
Am

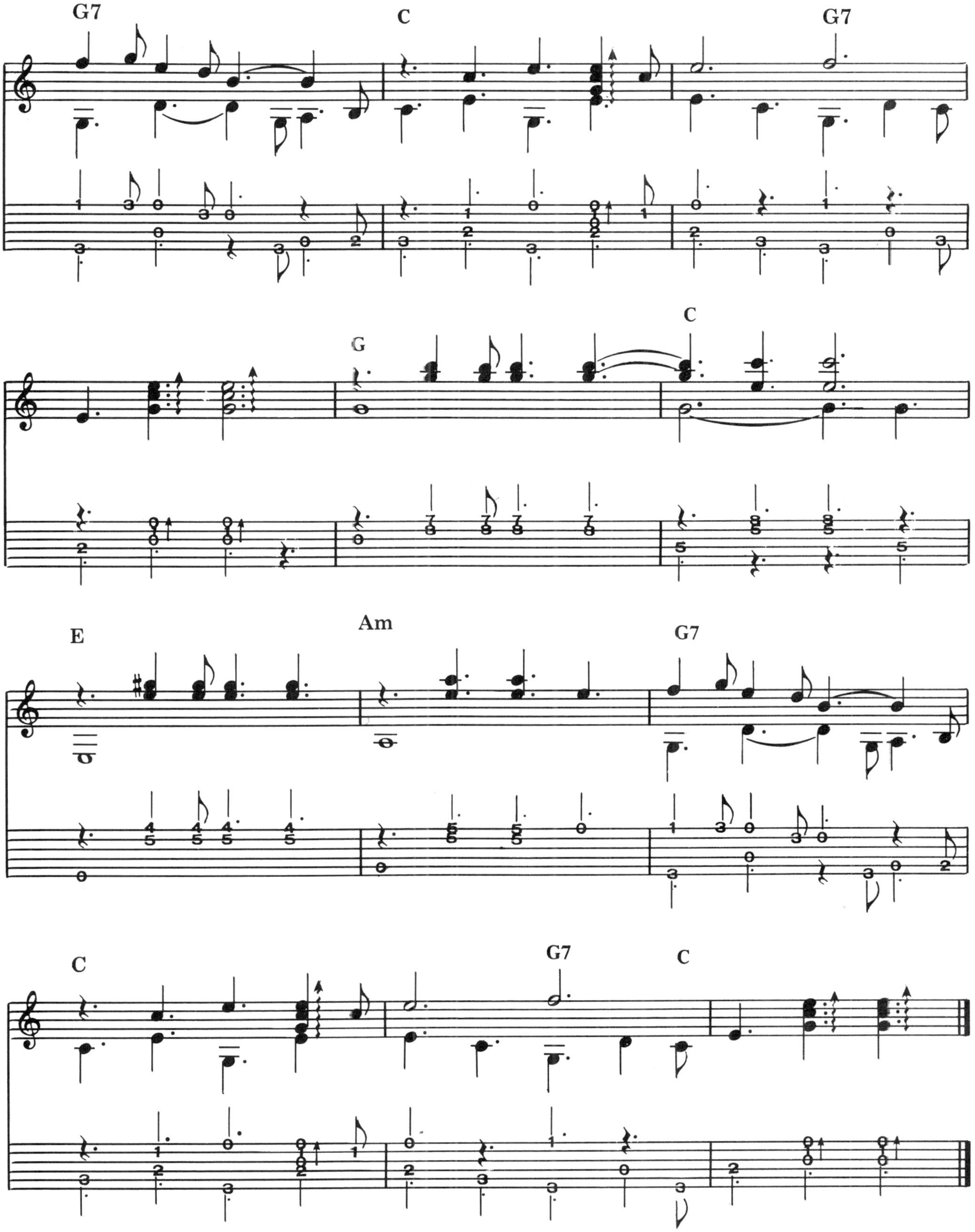
G7
C
G7
G
C
E
Am
G7
C
G7
C

Blind Lemon Jefferson

Rabbit Foot Blues

This is perhaps Lemon's guitar masterpiece. It is an imitation of the old boogie-woogie piano that was popular then. Play in open-G tuning: (D G D G B D).

Even the old Paramount advertisement makes a plug for the guitar accompaniment. This is a very unique way to play in open-G. The Mississippi Delta bluesmen used this tuning frequently but with a different effect. Leadbelly apparently learned a great deal from Lemon and the theme presented in the first few measures appears in much of his music.

Try to hear the original as it is one of the great recorded blues.

Lemon played many other blues in open-G tuning using different runs and different timings. This piece should help you with the others.

The guitar introduction, as well as the accompaniment to the second verse, has been transcribed.

Rabbit Foot Blues
Introduction

Verse

Strike strings
muffled

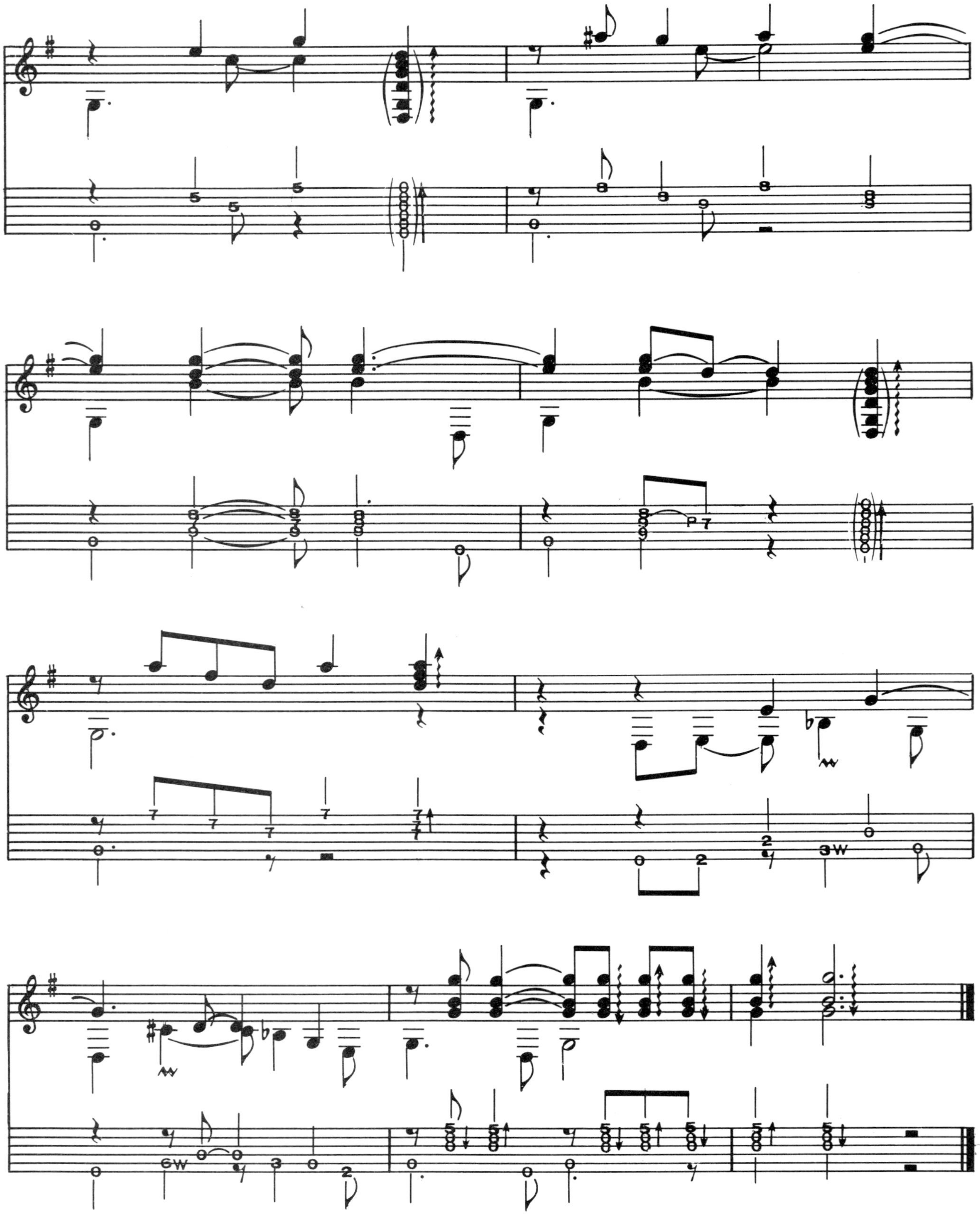

Blues jumped a rabbit, run him one
  solid mile.
Blues jumped a rabbit, run him one
  solid mile.
The rabbit fell down, cryin' like a
  natural child.

Well, it seem like you're hungry,
  honey, come and lunch with me.
Seem like you're hungry, honey,
  come and lunch with me.
I wanna stop these nice-lookin'
  women from worryin' me.

I have Uneeda Biscuits gal, and a
  half-pint of gin.
(Have) Uneeda Biscuits and half a
  pint of gin.
The gin is mighty fine, but them
  biscuits (are a) little too thin.

Baby tell me somethin', bout the
  meatless and wheatless day.
I wanna know about the meatless
  and wheatless day.
This not bein' my home, I don't
  think I could stay.

I tried corn flour and I mean I
  declare it was strong.
Thought I'd try corn flour, I mean
  I declare it was strong.
People feed me cornbread, I just
  can't stick around long.

Got an airplane, baby now we're
  gonna get a submarine.
An airplane baby, now we're gonna
  get a submarine.
Gonna get that Kaiser, and we'll be
  (seldom seen/sailin' clean*)

Mmm, hitch me to your buggy mama,
  drive me like a mule.
Hitch me to your buggy, drive me
  like a mule.
(And I'm/End up) goin' home with
  the sugar**, I ain't much hard to
  be fooled.

*If Lemon sings "sailin' clean" rather than "seldom seen" or even some other phrase, "clear" is probably used to connote smartness in appearance or correctness of procedure, in keeping with its customary slang usage.

**"Sugar" is generally used to mean either "money" or as an obscene reference to female genitalia.

Hot Dogs

Here is another popular Ragtime instrumental that has been recorded under several different titles by Leadbelly, Mance Lipscomb and many others. It is played in regular tuning in the key of C. The syncopation is the hardest part of this piece and is quite different from North Carolina syncopation. Your ear puts in many notes that the guitar doesn't play. I suppose this is a sign of a good arrangement.

"Hot Dogs" is reminiscent of African guitar playing as recorded by Hugh Tracey and issued by Decca on their *Guitars of Africa*. It also vaguely reminds me of Rev. Davis's "Candyman." The timing is quite different but the fingering is almost identical.

This is another piece that must be heard in order to grasp its total effect. I've transcribed the first three choruses.

Hot Dogs

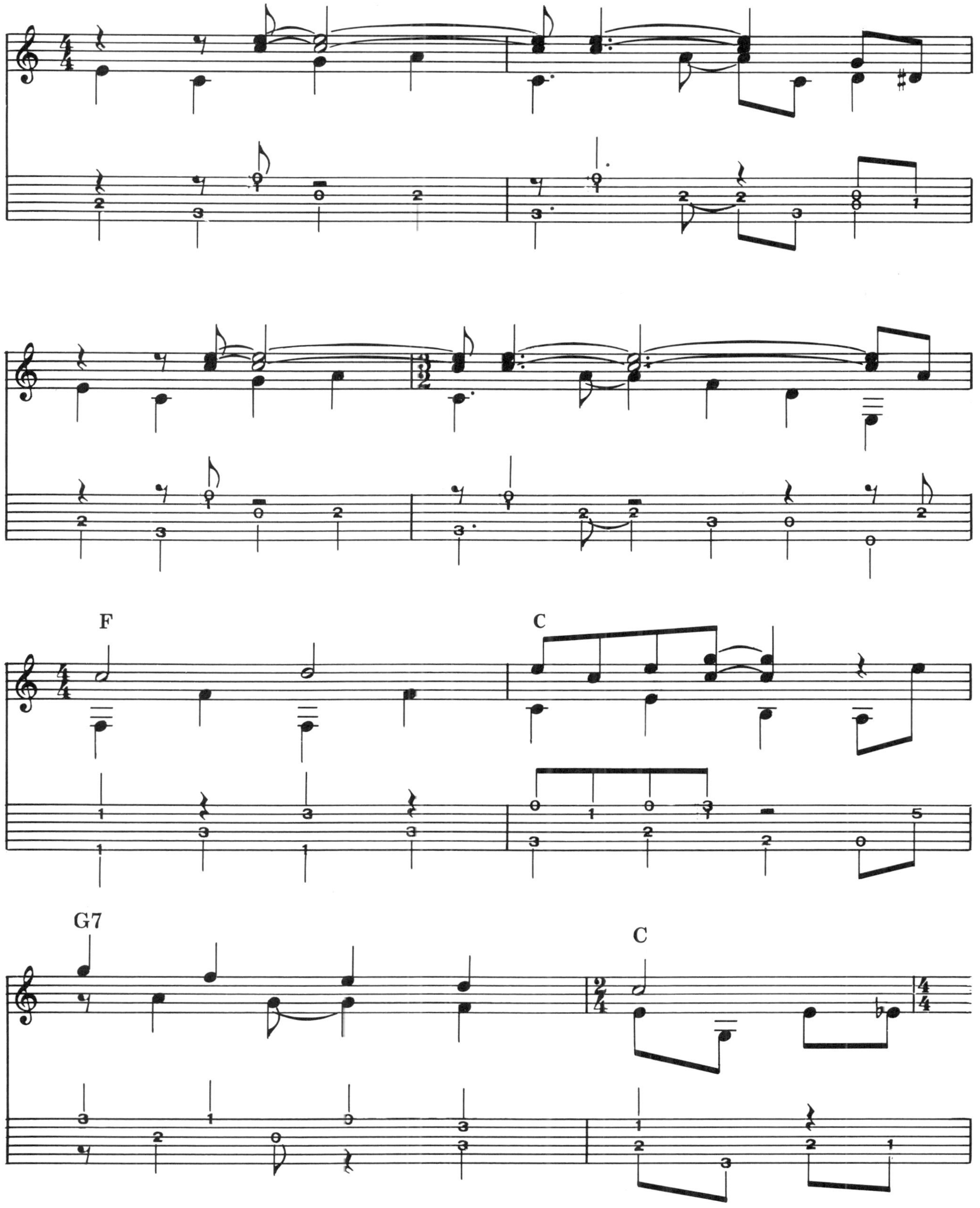
F
C
G7
C

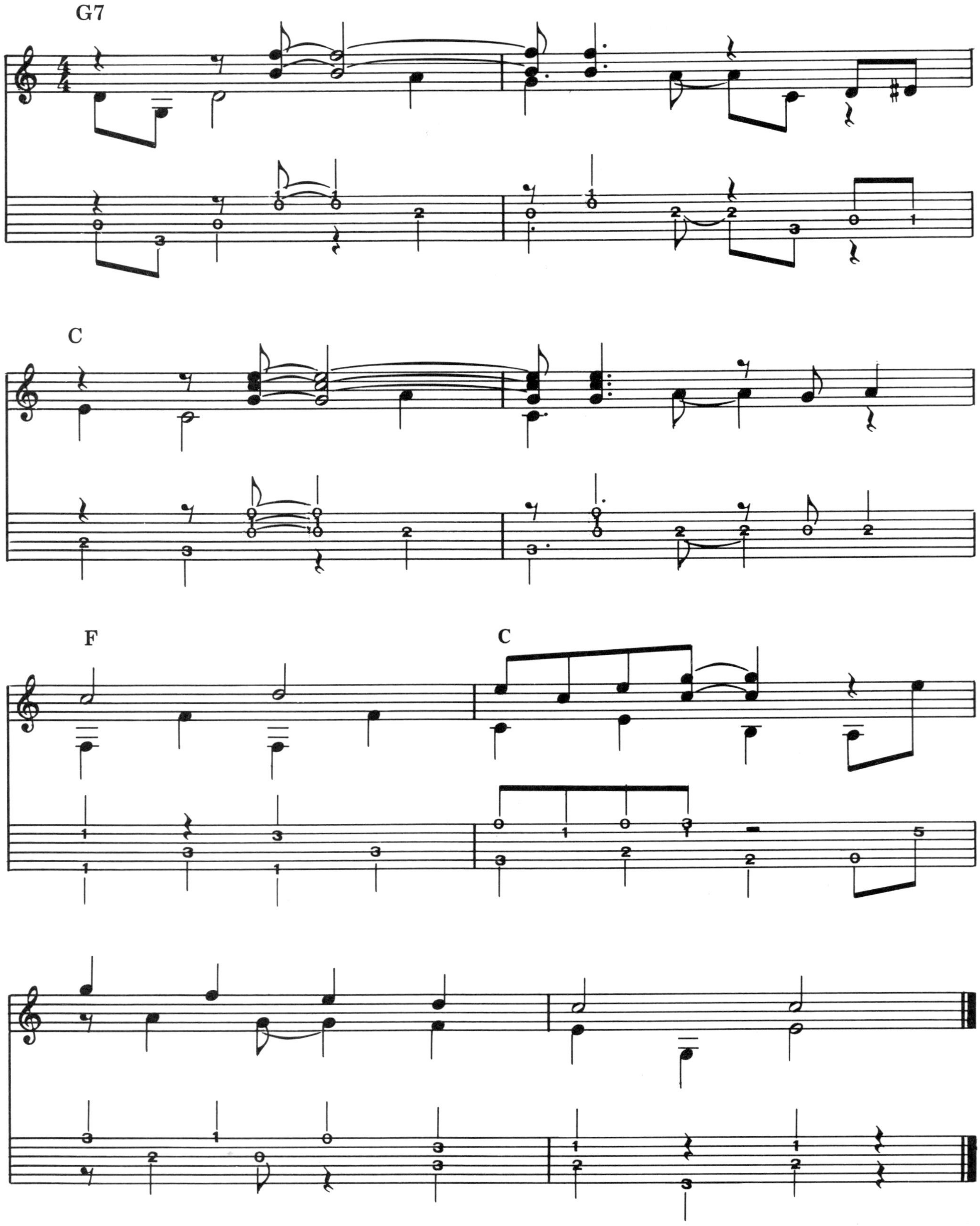
G7
C
F
C

Black Horse Blues

Here is Blind Lemon's unique version of the famous "Pony Blues." It reminds me of many of Gary Davis's gospel pieces like "Trying to Get Home," "Great Change since I Been Born," and "Pure Religion." "Black Horse Blues" is played in the key of C using regular tuning. Like "Hot Dogs" it is difficult in its timing and syncopation.

The arrangement begins with a phrase associated with "St. Louis Tickle" or "Buddy Bolden's Blues." It is a good example of how one set of words developed many different types of musical backing. Most of the songs presented in this volume were used as dance music. Therefore, the lyrics were not as important as the music. All of the songs have strongly accented rhythms and you should strive to bring out this quality in the music.

The first guitar break has been transcribed.

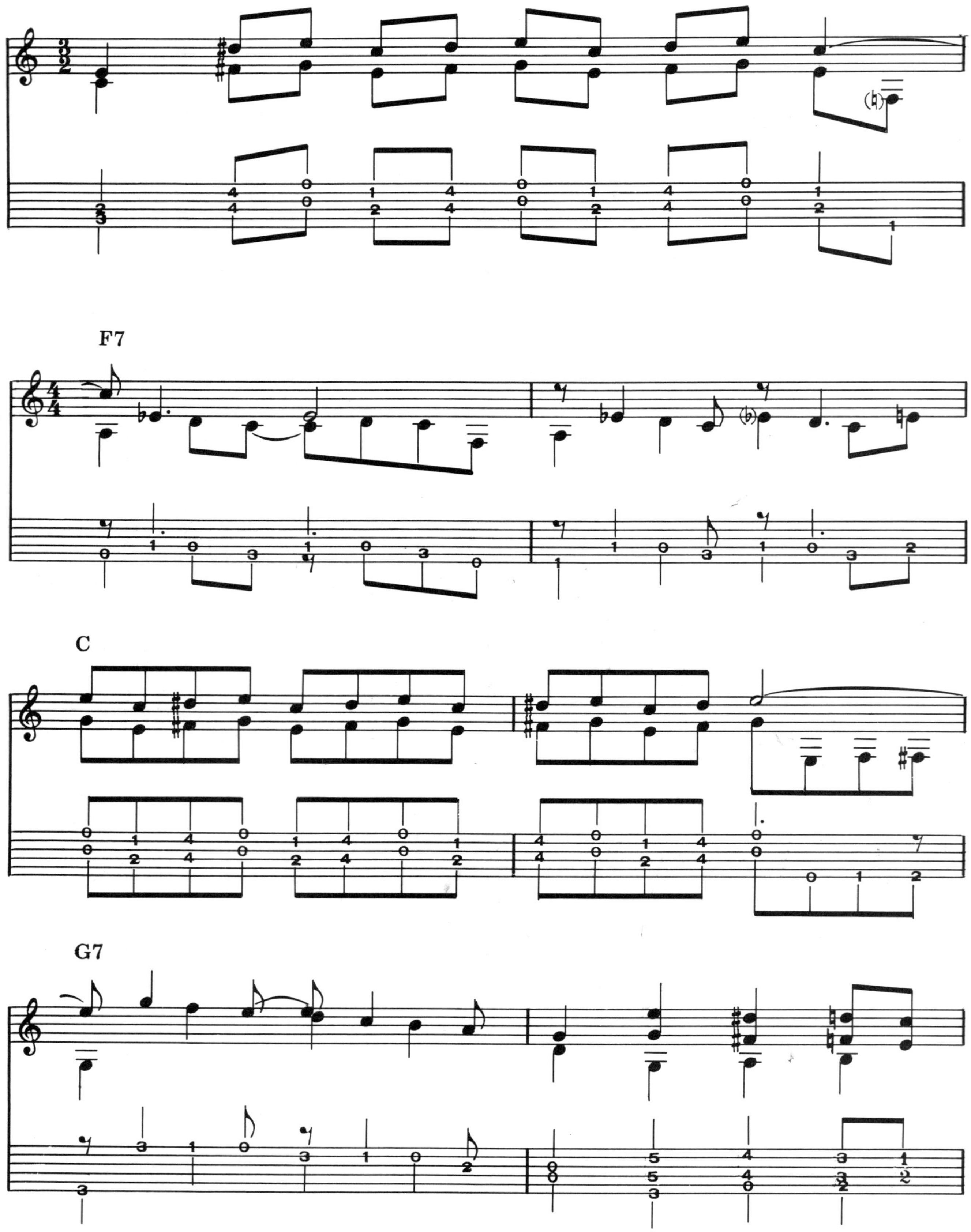
F7
C
G7

*Tell me, what time do the trains
come through your town?
I wanna know what time do the
trains come through your town.
I wanna laugh and talk with a
long-haired teasin' brown.*

*One goes south at eight, and it's
one goes north at nine.
One goes south at eight, one goes
north at nine.
I got an hour to talk with that long-
haired brown of mine.*

*Go get my black horse and saddle
up my grey mare.
Go get my black horse and saddle
up my grey mare.
I'm goin' off to my good gal, she's
in the world somewhere.*

*I can't count the times I was so
dissatisfied.
I can't count the times I was so
dissatisfied.
Sugar, the blues ain't on me but
things ain't goin' on right.*

Cordially Yours
Blind Blake

Blind Blake

Black Dog Blues

"He was a *sporting* guitar player . . . he sure could play. These are the words of Rev. Gary Davis—one of the greatest blues guitarists to come out of the South. He rarely complements other old-timers but his estimation of Blake's guitar playing is of the highest.

"Blind Blake was a house musician for one of the major companies from 1926 until the Depression, and hence one of the most prominent East Coast stylists of the 1920s. A resident of Patterson, Georgia, where Blake has relatives, reports that he was a native of Tampa who customarily played in northern Florida and southern Georgia."

—Stephen Calt, Nick Perls and Michael Stewart from the album notes to *East Coast Blues* (Yazoo Records, 1013).

Rev. Davis recalls talk that Blake's death happened in New York City in the 1930s but this, he says, is hearsay. The dearth of information about Blake seems quite incredible. He was the best-remembered recording artist of the twenties, yet few people can recall where he came from or where he played.

His style is a fantastically complicated one. It is highly syncopated, relying on a difficult right-hand technique. Again, Rev. Davis is the only artist I have ever heard who could faithfully duplicate this sound. I asked him to explain the right-hand movements and he merely said, "It's your basic touch that makes the roll. . . ain't all that hard!"

But in order to reproduce Blake's sound you must roll your bass and think of your guitar as a piano. In most of Blake's pieces there is an evident Ragtime quality. Even his blues sound like a slow piano blues. Only "Police Dog Blues" seems to use the guitar as a guitar.

Despite the many thousands of race records that were made, "Police Dog Blues" seems to be the only old 78 where harmonics can be heard.

The other four tunes of Blake's that appear here represent his style in his favorite keys: C and G. He rarely played in A and to hear a tune of his in E is even more unusual.

The "extra hot" guitar of Blake was advertised in the old days as his famous "piano sounding guitar."

His singing technique was not one good for "hard blues." He delivered his words as a counterpoint to the guitar accompaniment. Listen to "Policy Blues," which is another rare arrangement in its approach. He casually sang his blues or raps with almost a comic approach. The best example of this is in his "Rope Stretchin' Blues."

Luckily, in the last few years Blind Blake has become very popular with up-and-coming new guitarists. This has led to the reissue of many of his records. In Europe there have been a half-dozen LPs released that are now out of print. America has begun to reissue Blake's material and hopefully these records will be available for a long time.

Try to approach Blake's guitar pieces with the greatest patience. They are indeed hard to master. You should definitely hear the originals as this will help a great deal. I also suggest you play these tunes without fingerpicks. Fingerpicks would prevent you from getting a smooth, bouncy, Ragtime texture.

This is a typical Blind Blake blues accompaniment. It is played in regular tuning in the key of C. The piano sound is achieved by doubling the bass. The bass alternates and double-times throughout all of his songs.

Blake's most famous blues in C is "Early Morning Blues," which has not yet been reissued. "Black Dog Blues" can be heard on a Biograph disc solely devoted to Blake songs. You should hear many of his pieces to get an idea of what he is trying to achieve. This is another artist who was a much better guitarist than singer. He was the first of the great "studio musicians."

The guitar introduction and accompaniment to the first verse have been transcribed.

Black Dog Blues
Introduction

First Verse

Let me tell you, mama, what that
  black dog done to me.
Let me tell you, mama, what that
  black dog done to me.
He cheated me from my regular, now
  he's after my used-to-be.

Black dog, black dog, you caused
  me to weep and moan.
  (Repeat line)
You cause me to leave my, sweet old
  happy home.

Black dog, black dog, you forever on
  my mind.
  (Repeat line)
If you only let me see my baby one
  more time.

So long black dog, I'm quittin' your
  hard luck line.
  (Repeat line)
'Cause you got me so blue, keep
  'bout to love her sometime.

Policy Blues

This is a very unusual Ragtime blues that has the feeling of bluegrass music. It sounds as if Blake could be using a flatpick but I tend to think he is using only his thumb and index finger. It is played in regular tuning in the key of G. I have transcribed the accompaniment to the first verse as well as the guitar break.

Instead of an alternating bass, a quick succession of bass runs are linked together to create a cohesive guitar part.

Policy Blues

First Verse

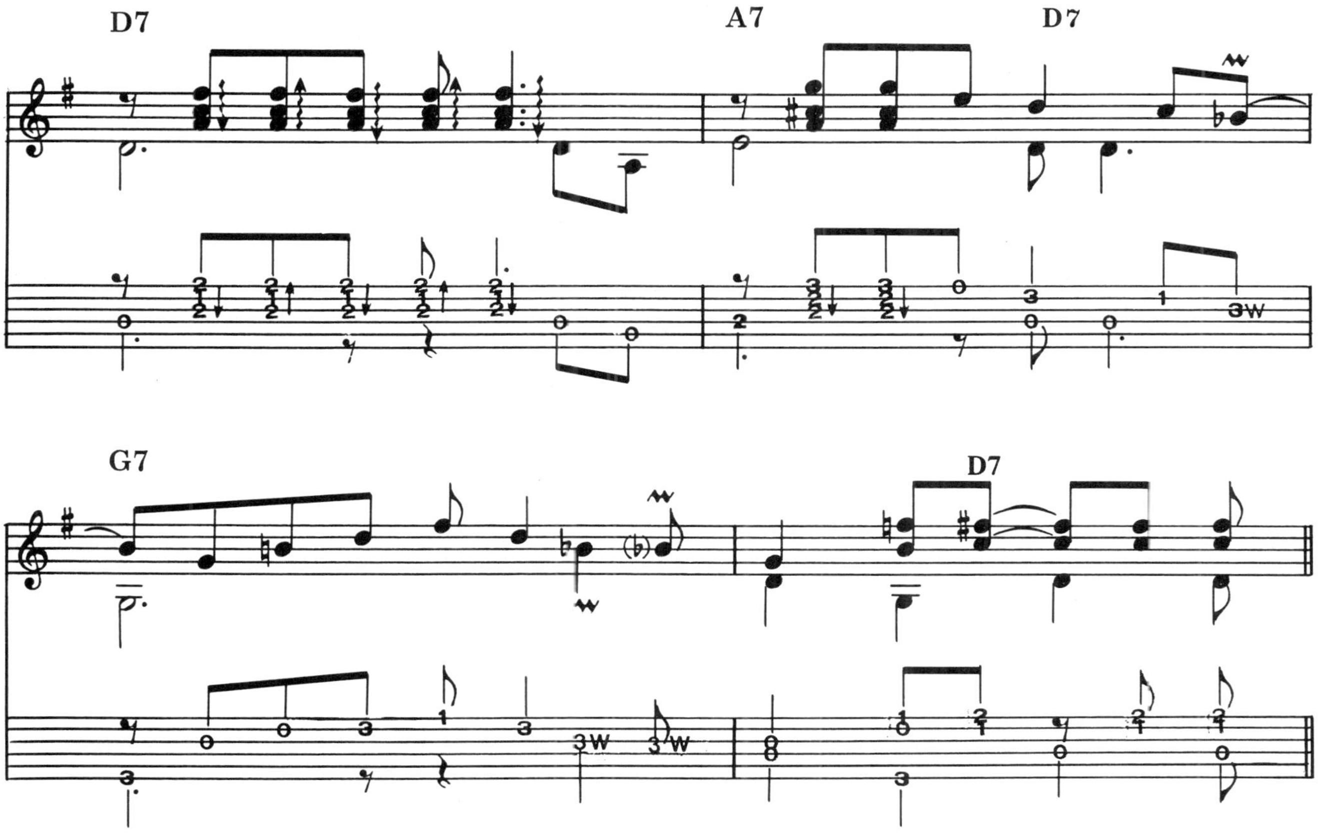

Guitar Break

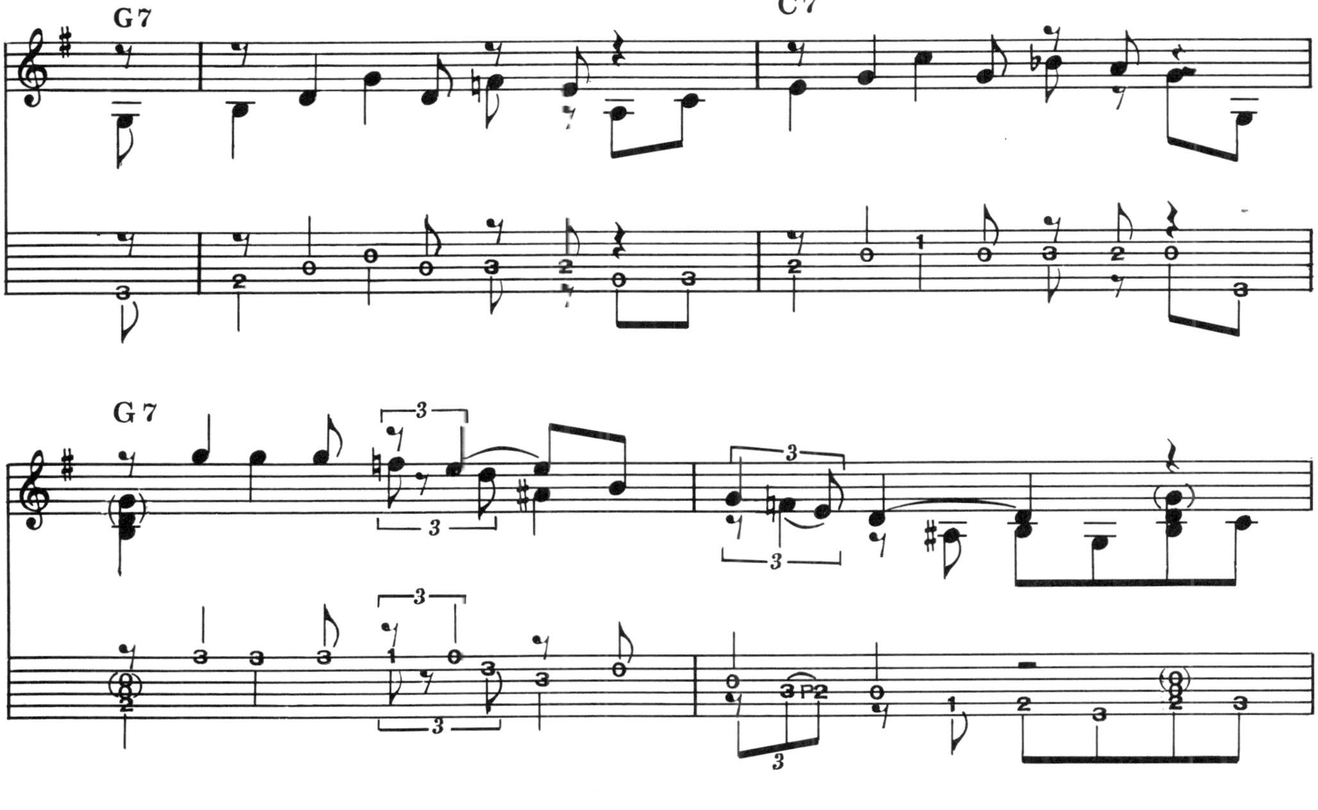

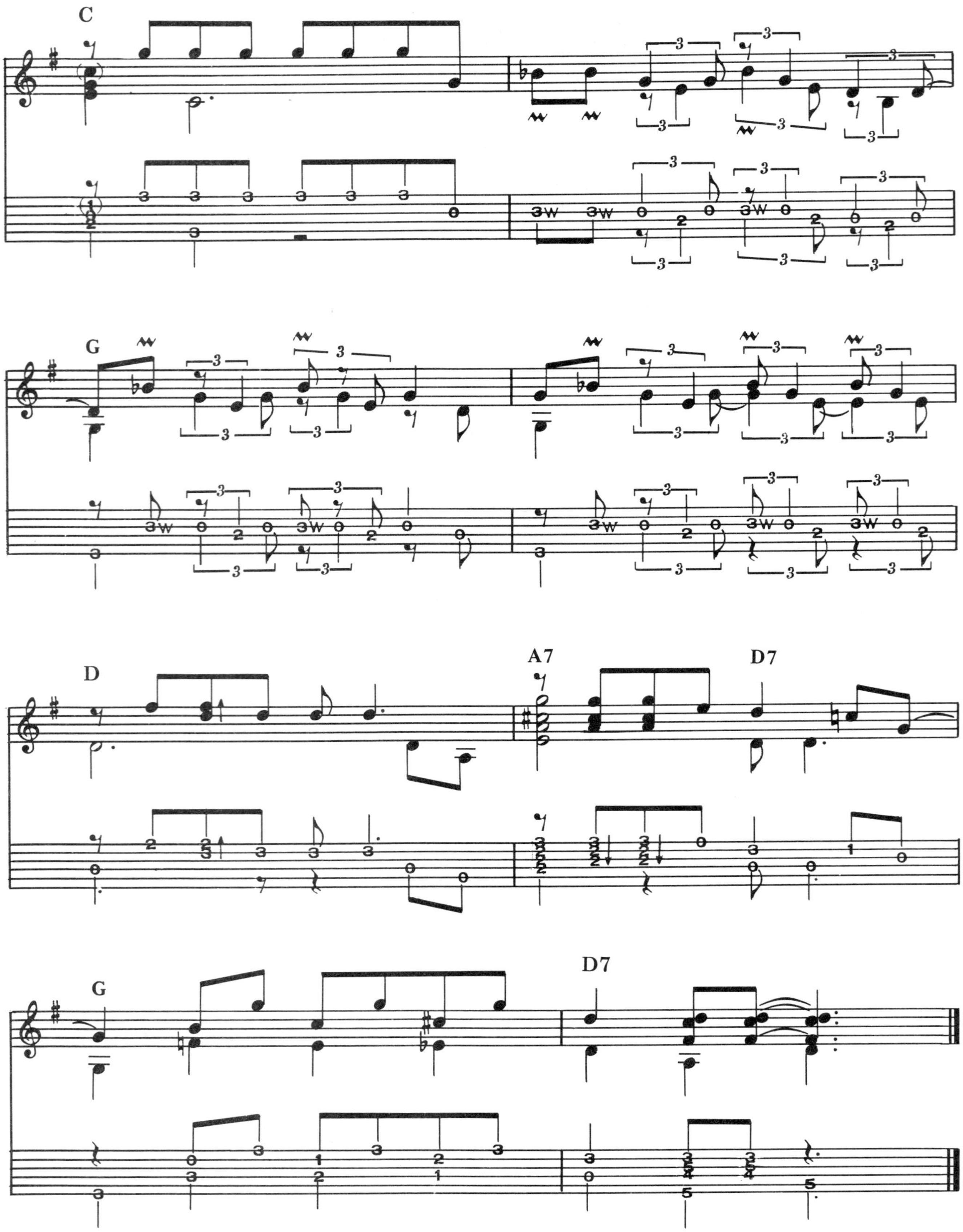
C
G
D
A7
D7
G
D7

*Number, numbers, 'bout to drive me
  mad.*
*Number, numbers, 'bout to drive me
  mad.*
*Thinking about the money that I
  should have had.*

*I dreamed last night the woman I
  love was dead.*
  (Repeat line)
*If I had not played with dead row,
  I would come out ahead.*

*I acted a fool and played all three six
  nine.*
  (Repeat line)
Lost my money and the gal of mine.

*I played on clear house, couldn't
  make a grade.*
  (Repeat line)
*Lord, pick up the money that I
  should have made.*

I beg my baby, let me in her door.
  (Repeat line)
*Want to put my twenty-five, fifty-
  five, seventy-five in her seven-
  seventeen twenty-four.*

*I walked fifteen-fifty and sixty-
  one.*
  (Repeat line)
*I'm gonna keep playing policy 'til
  some good luck come.*

That Will Never Happen No More

This is a great Ragtime song with some rather strange lyrics. It is played in regular tuning in the key of G and has many of Blake's trademarks. The bass alternates as well as jumps time to give that piano sound. In this tune you feel that Blake is playing "dirty." He is hitting two treble notes instead of one and the result is a fuller sound, not the clean sound that Mississippi John Hurt developed.

I have transcribed the first break which is similar to the accompaniment.

That Will Never Happen No More

That Will Never Happen No More

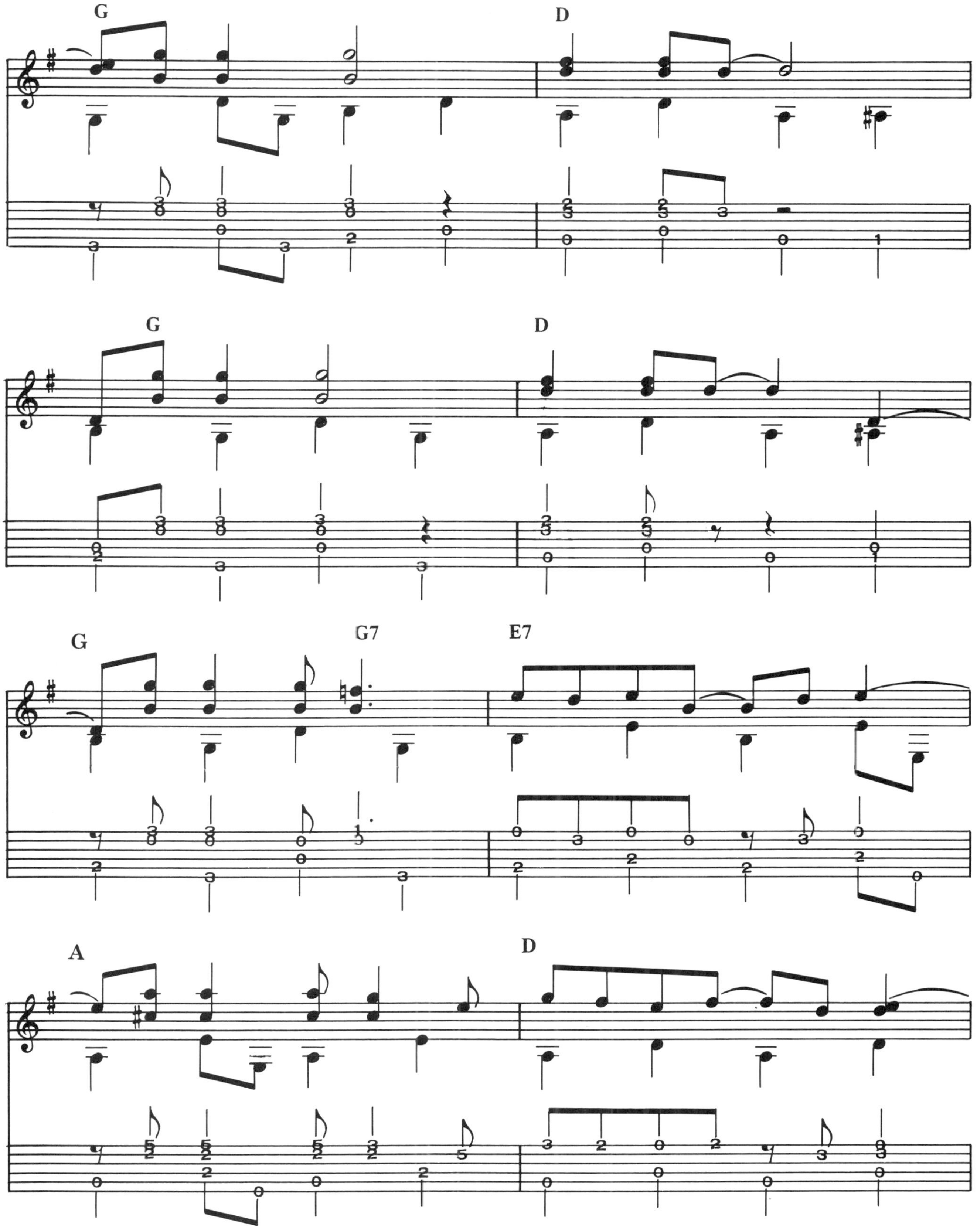
G
D
G
D
G
G7
E7
A
D

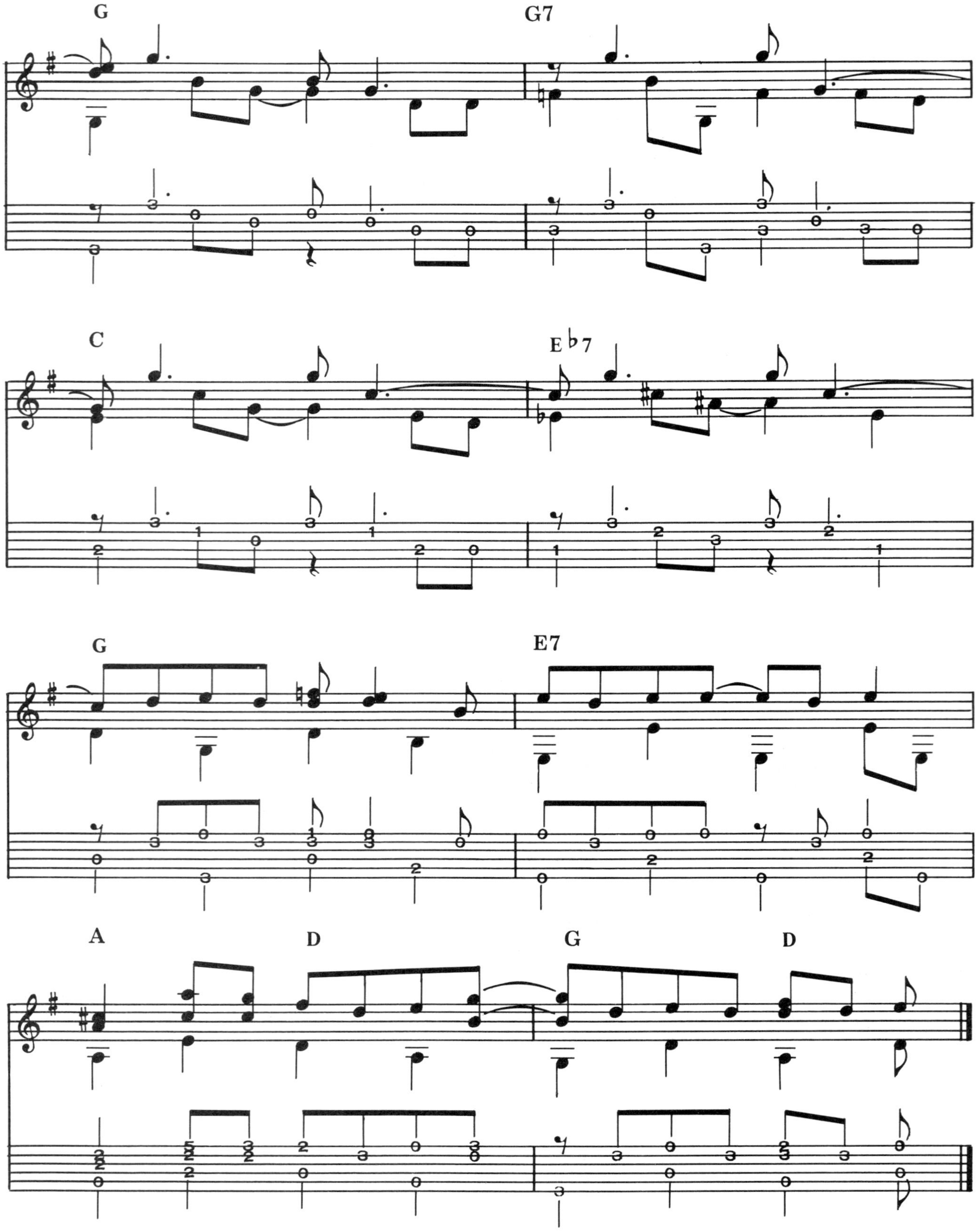
G
G7
C
E♭7
G
E7
A
D
G
D

I met a girl at the cabaret,
Said, "Pretty papa I'm goin' your
    way."
Her man know what it all about.
Waiting at home just to throw me out.
Broke my nose, split my chin.
"Don't let me catch you here again."
He whipped me from the kitchen
    back to the door.
He beat me with the chair till my
    head got sore.

Chorus:
That'll never happen no more.
That'll never happen no more.

The wind in Chicago, winter and
    fall,
Is what caused me to wear my
    overalls.
Got broke, was my fault.
Been used to eating porkchops and
    meat and salt.
I met a woman, just a pigmeat some.
Bit fatmouth-me followed her.
She pulled a gun, take my joint.
Didn't leave me hard on, didn't get
    sore.

Chorus

Wabash Rag

The chord progression used in this piece is typical of many Ragtime songs. I have transcribed the first guitar break as played by Blind Blake. Blind Boy Fuller recorded the same song under different titles. His most famous rendition was called "Rag Mama, Rag."

The guitar is in regular tuning and the piece is played in the key of C. The only tricky part is the right-hand technique which again uses the Blake jump that imitates the old pianos.

Wabash Rag

First Break

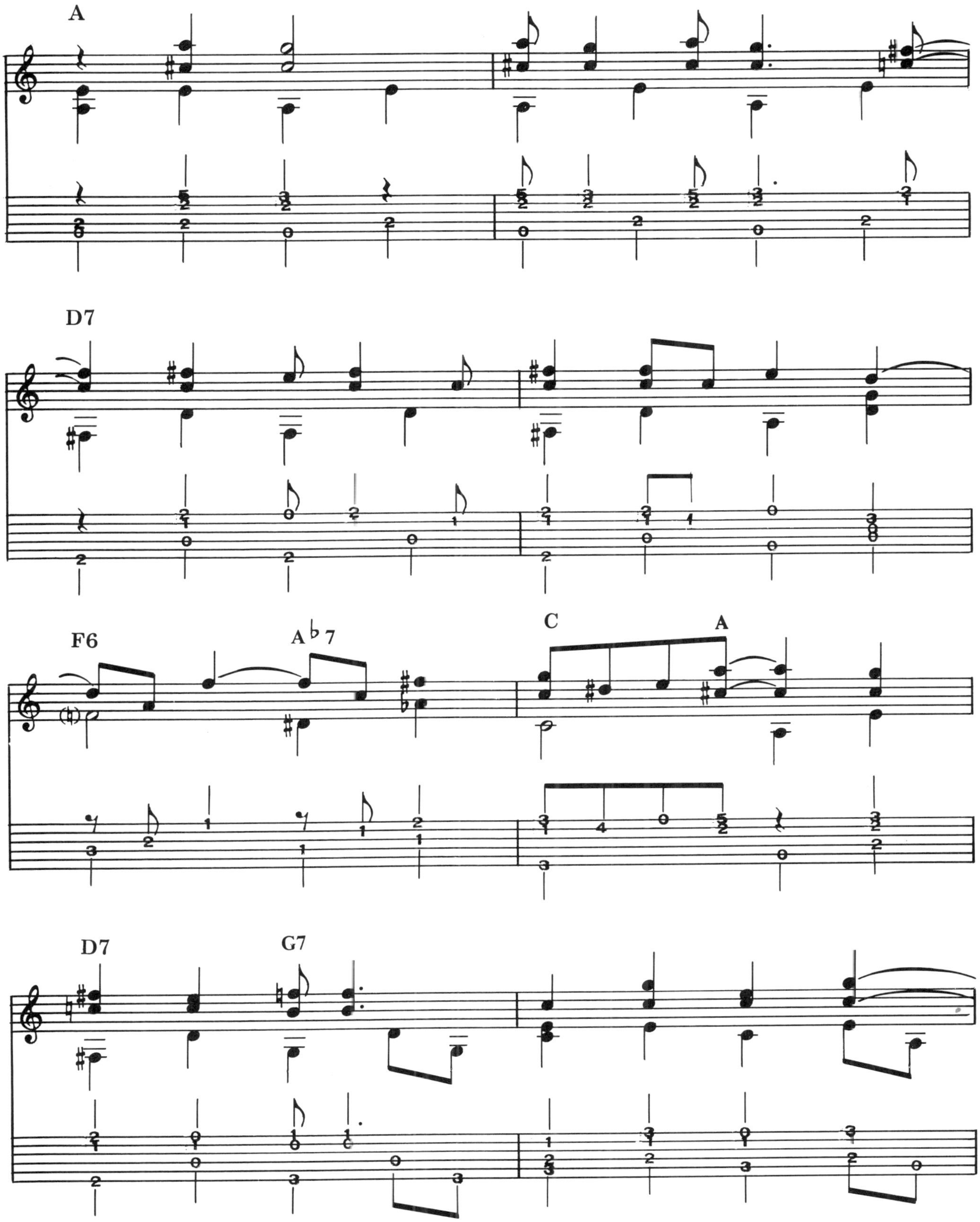
A
D7
F6
A♭7
C
A
D7
G7

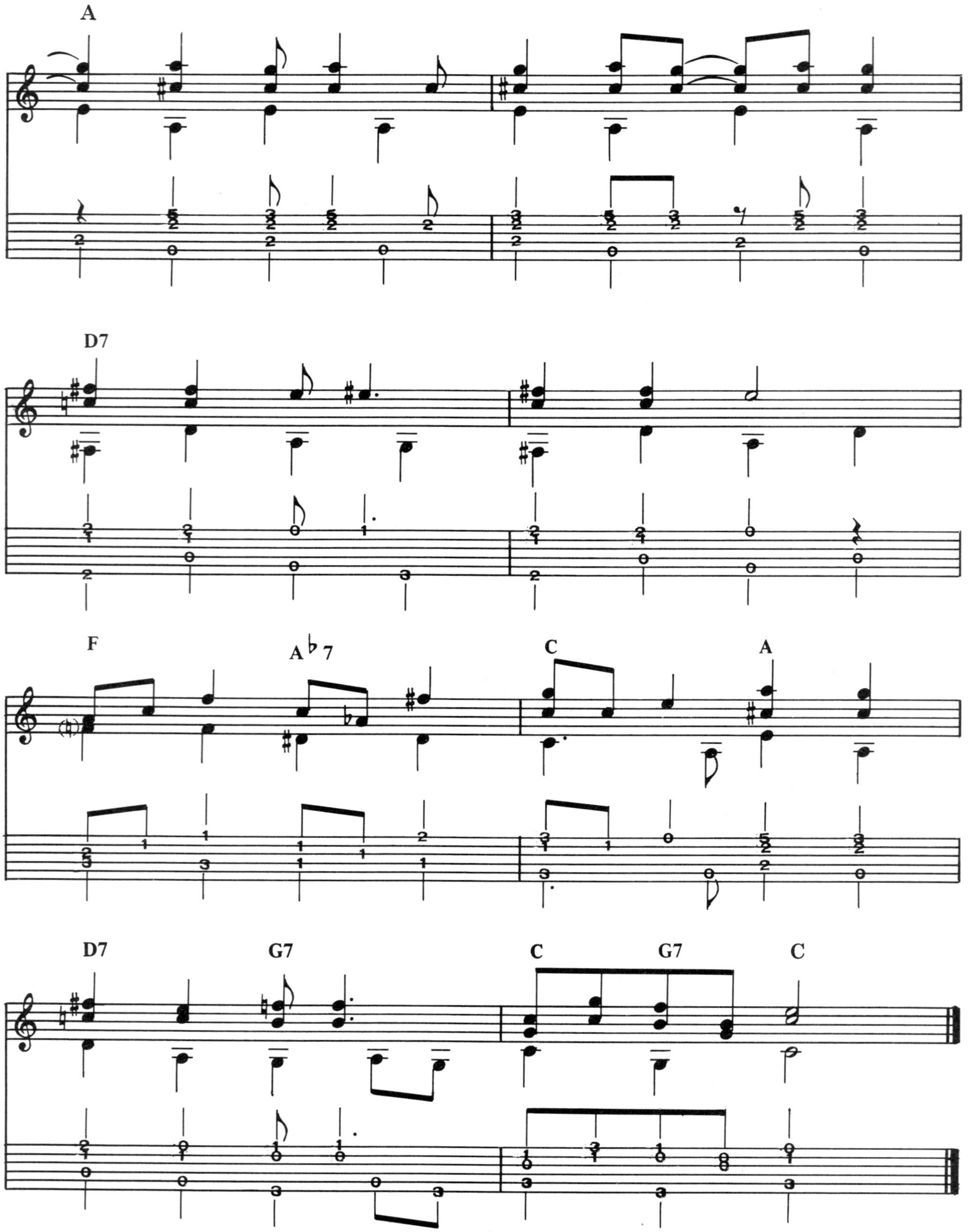
A
D7
F
A♭7
C
A
D7
G7
C
G7
C

Down south on Wabash Street,
Everybody you chance to meet,
Doing that rag, that Wabash Rag.

They're doing it night and day,
It will drive your blues away.
Doing that rag, that Wabash Rag.

Even the little kids that you meet,
In the alley, in the street,
Doing that rag, that Wabash Rag.

Grab me mama, hold me tight.
Let's mess around the rest of the
* night.*
Doing that rag, that Wabash Rag.

Throw your hands way up high,
Grab me mama, make me cry.
Doing that rag, that Wabash Rag.

People come from miles around.
Get on Wabash, break 'em down.
Doing that rag, that Wabash Rag.

Police Dog Blues

This is a rare Blake blues in open-E tuning (E B E G♯ B E) that uses harmonics. The bass also varies from steady alternating to half time (on beats one and three). I have transcribed the guitar introduction as well as four breaks. The accompaniment to the verses are just simplified versions of the breaks.

There is no difficult fingering but the timing is a little tricky.

It is interesting to compare this with Fuller's "Little Woman, You're So Sweet," which is played in open-D* but not as complex. Yet, "Police Dog Blues" does not sound intricate once you can play it fluidly.

*Since open-E and open-D tuning share the same pitch relationships a whole-step apart, tablature transcriptions of solos in either tuning are interchangeable.

Police Dog Blues

Introduction

First Break

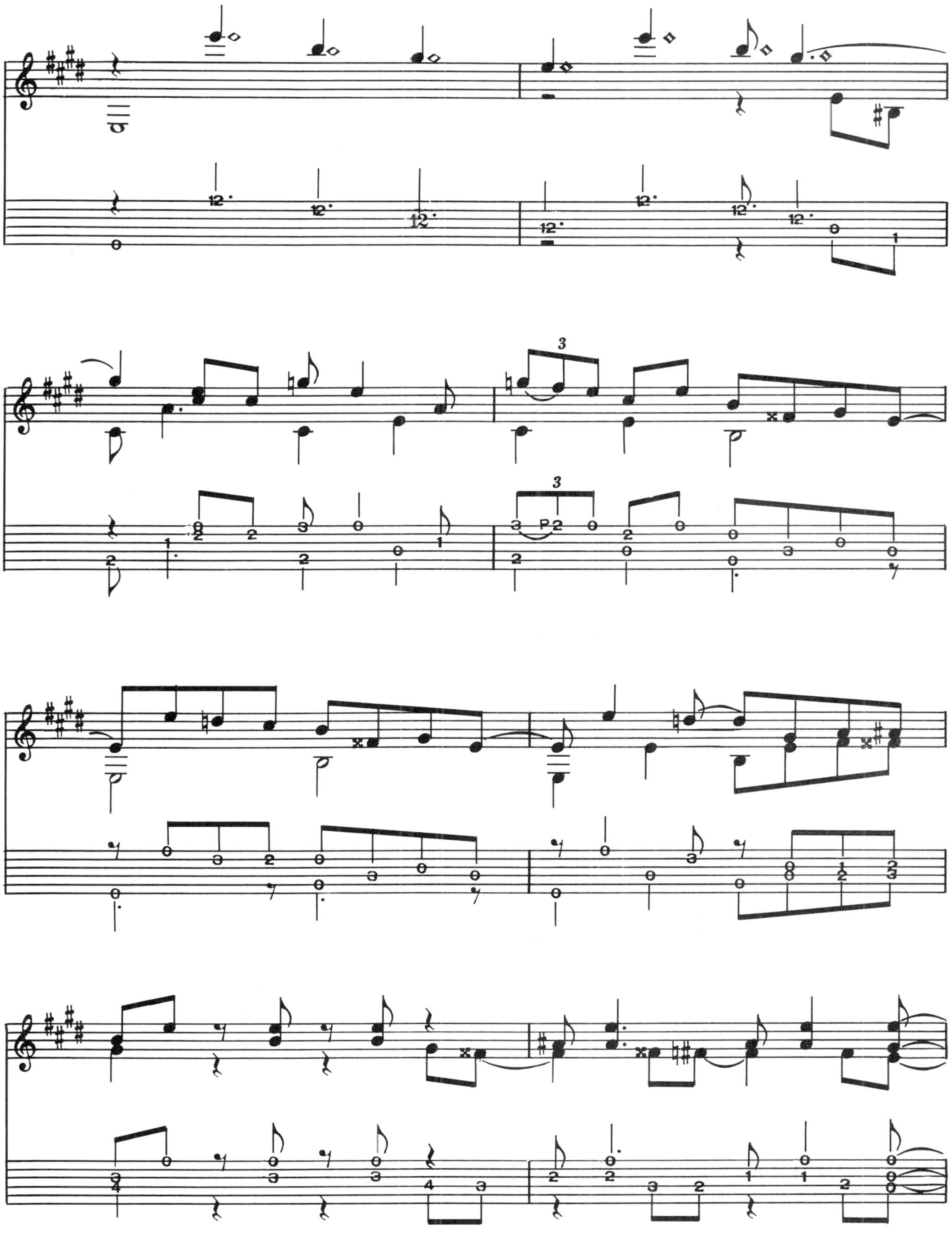

Second Break

Third Break

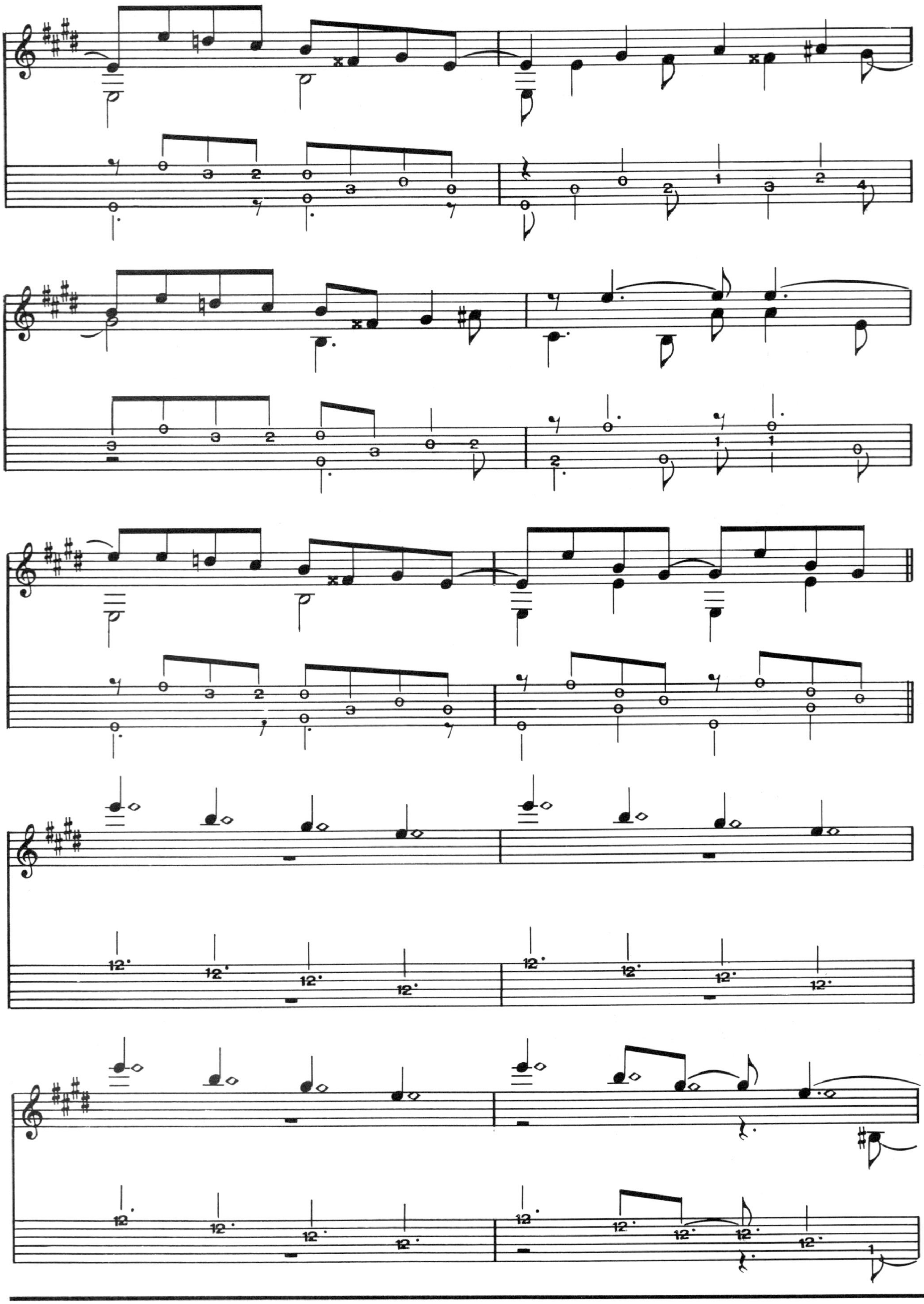

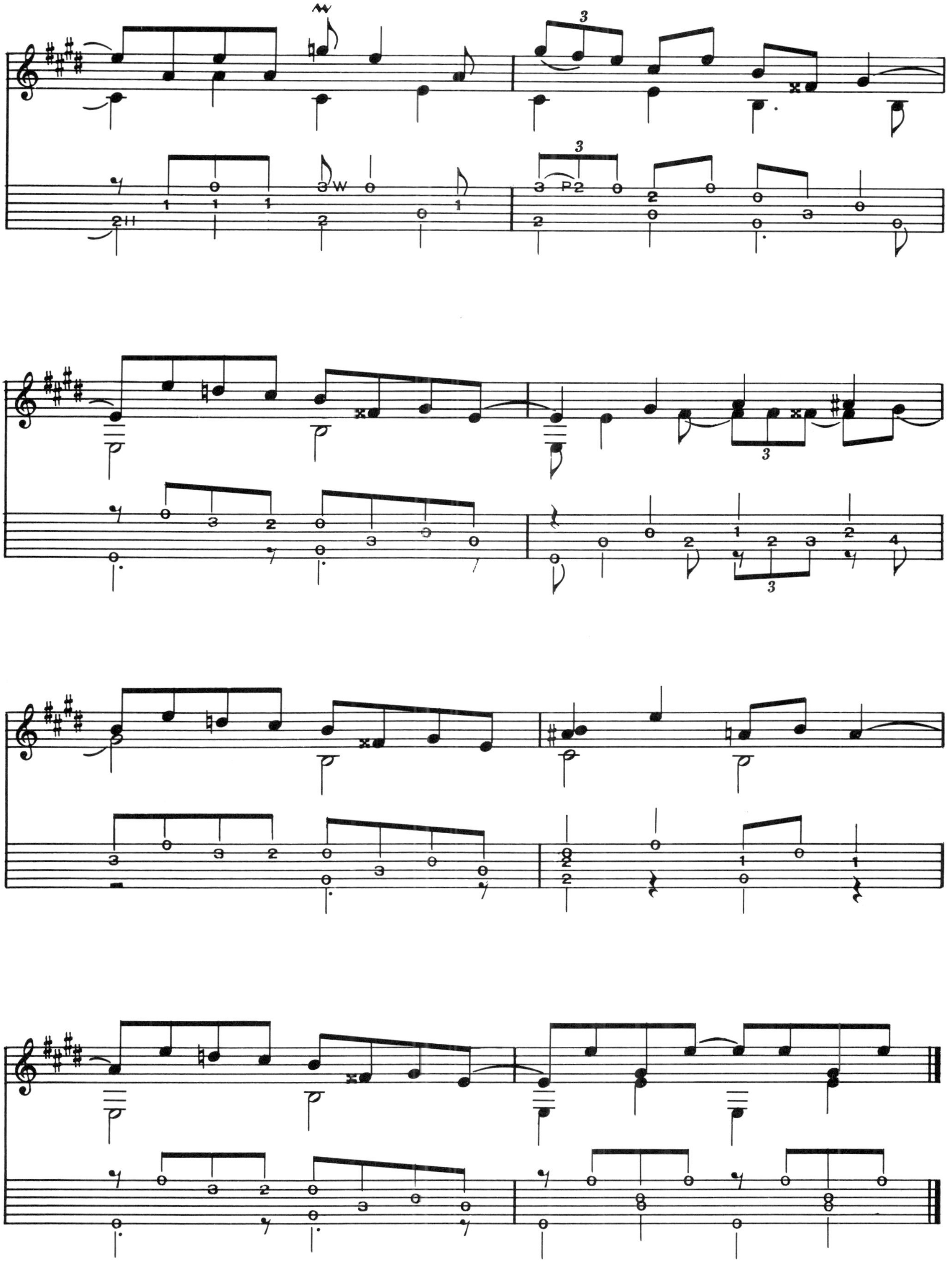

All my life I've been a travelin' man.
All my life I've been a travelin' man.
Staying alone and doing the best I can.

I shipped my trunk down to Tennes-
see.
    (Repeat line)
Hard to tell about a man like me.

I met a gal couldn't get her off my
mind.
    (Repeat line)
She passed me up, saying she didn't
like my kind.

I'm scared to bother around her
house at night.
    (Repeat line)
Got a police dog, craving for a fight.

His name is ramblin' when he gets
the chance.
    (Repeat line)
He leaves his mark on everybody's
pants.

Guess I'll travel, guest I'll let her be.
    (Repeat line)
Before she sics her police dog on me.

West Coast Blues

We end our study with Blake's famous "West Coast Blues." This was the first great guitar instrumental recorded and one of the most imitated. As in most Blake pieces the left-hand technique is not difficult. The right hand, which should take you some time to master, is what produces his unique sound.

The chording of the C chord in this tune is interesting.

"West Coast Blues" is played in regular tuning in the key of C. I have transcribed the guitar introduction as well as the first chorus and variation.

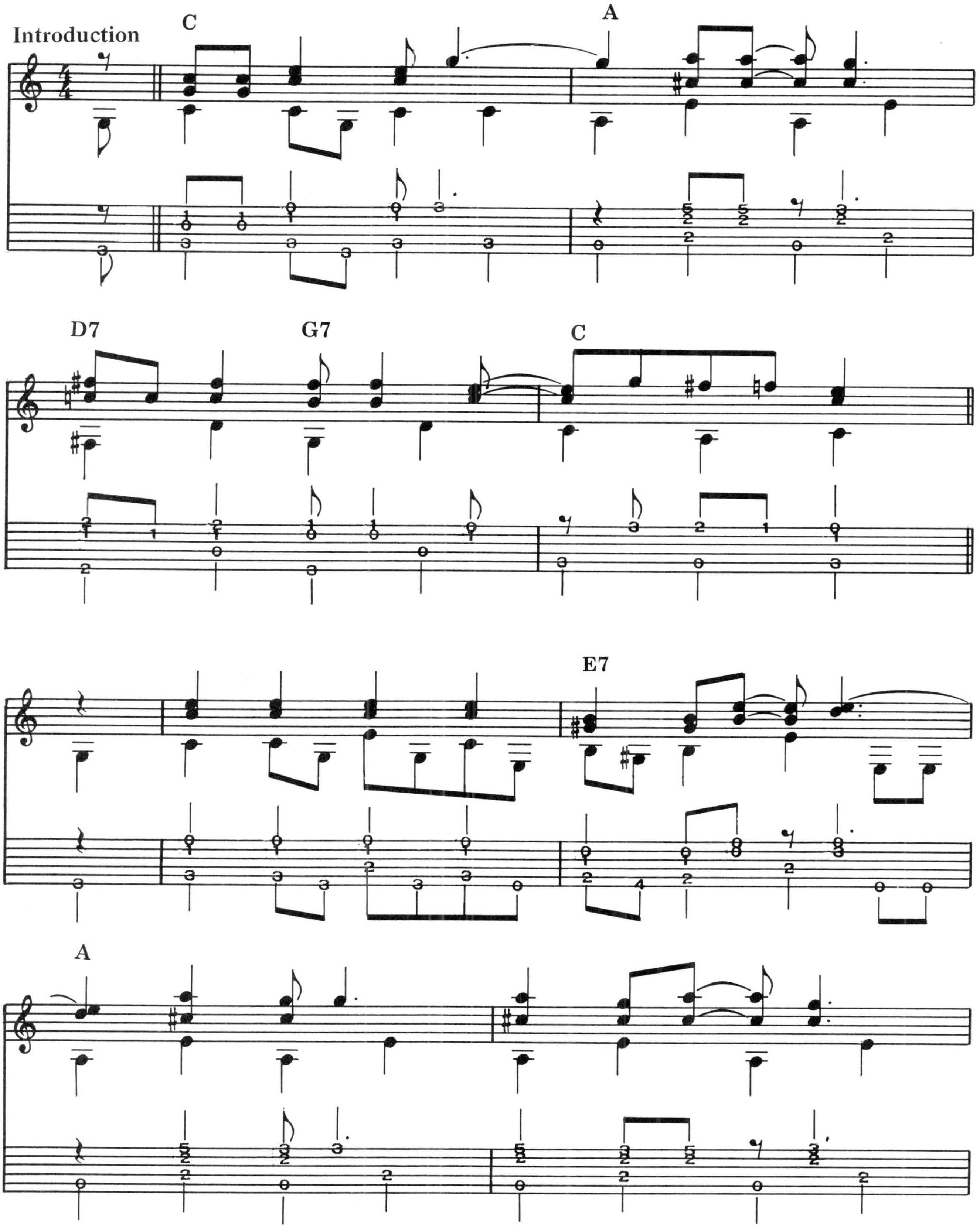
Introduction
C
A
D7
G7
C
E7
A

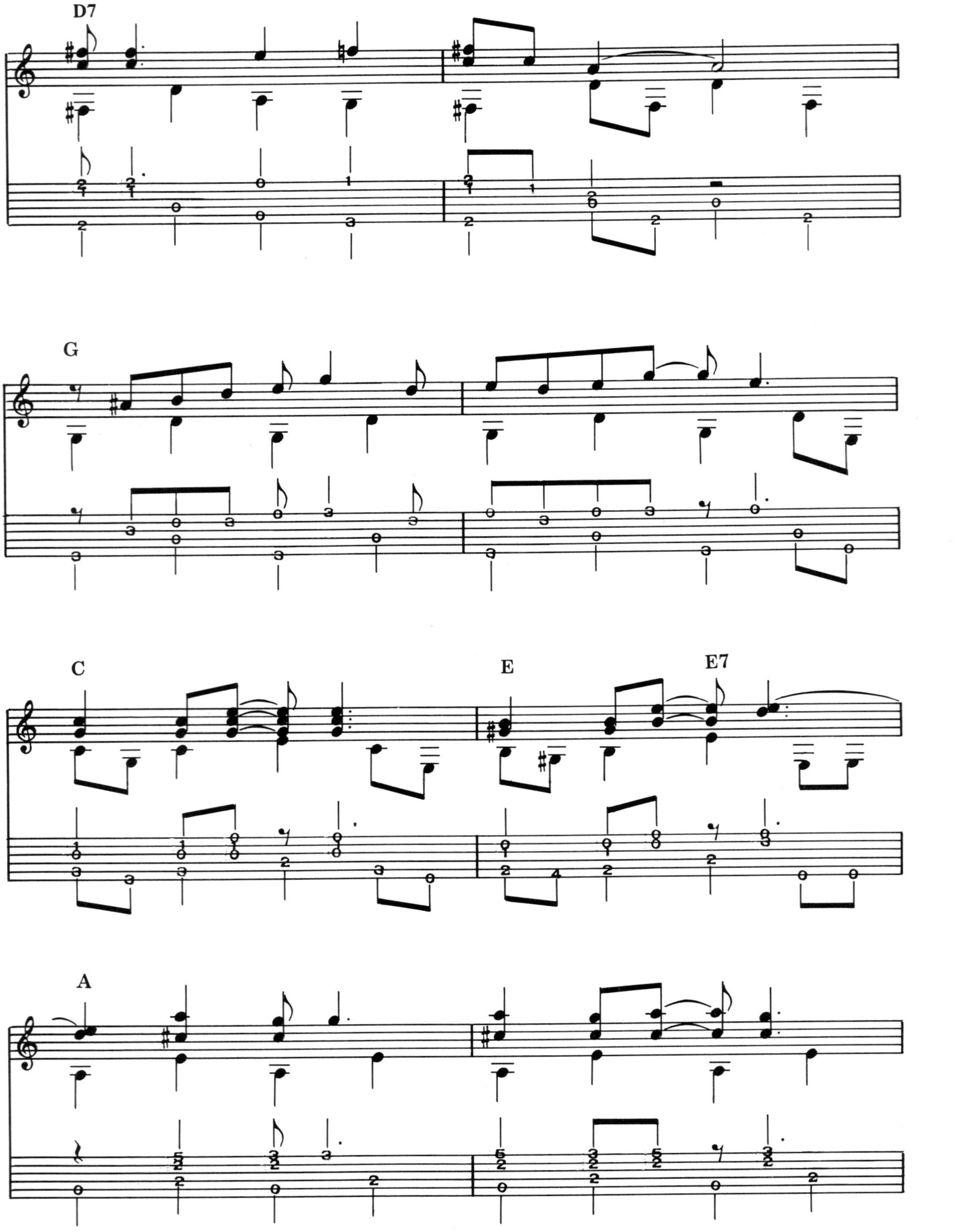
D7
G
C
E
E7
A

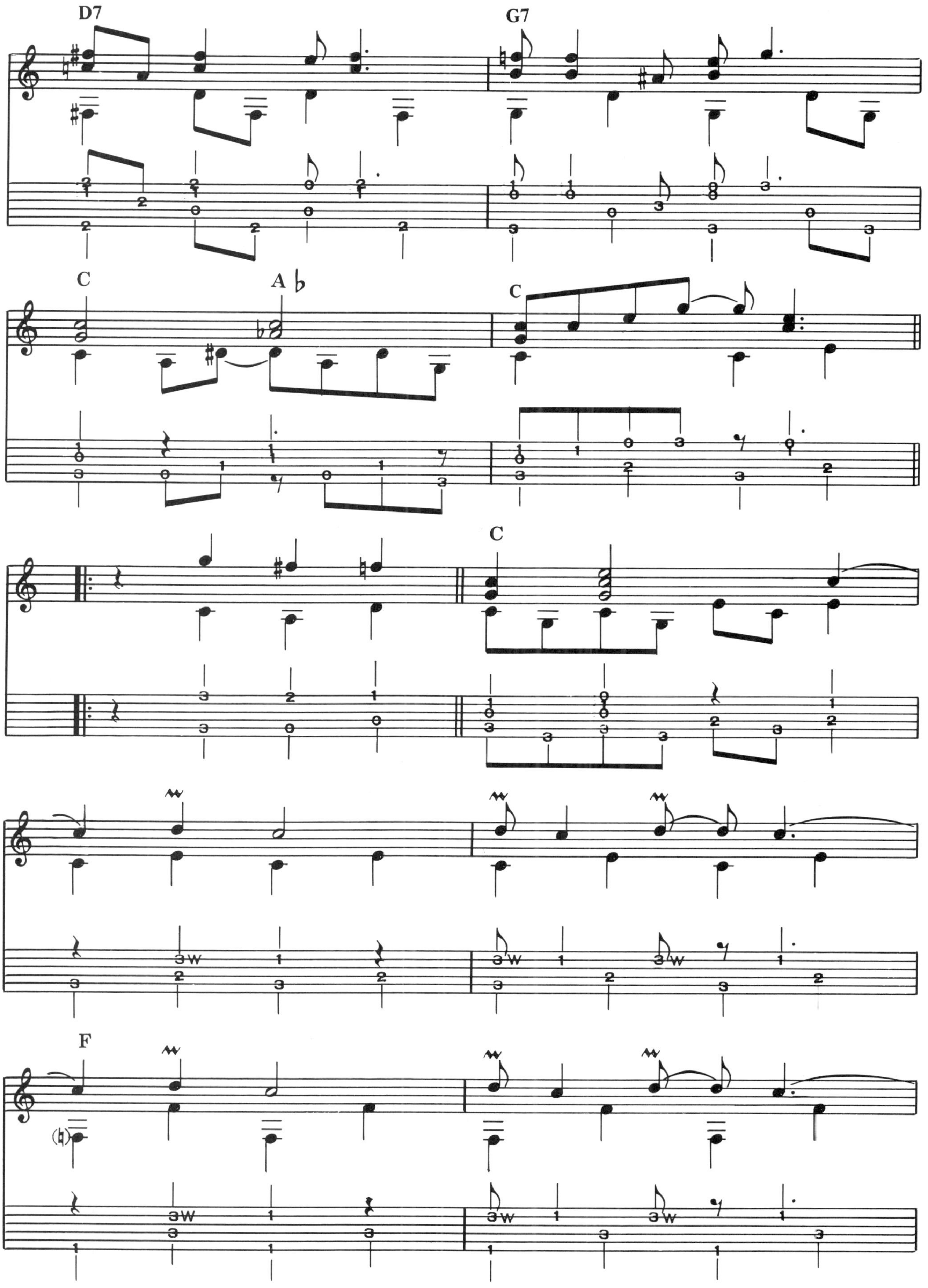
D7
G7
C
A♭
C
C
F

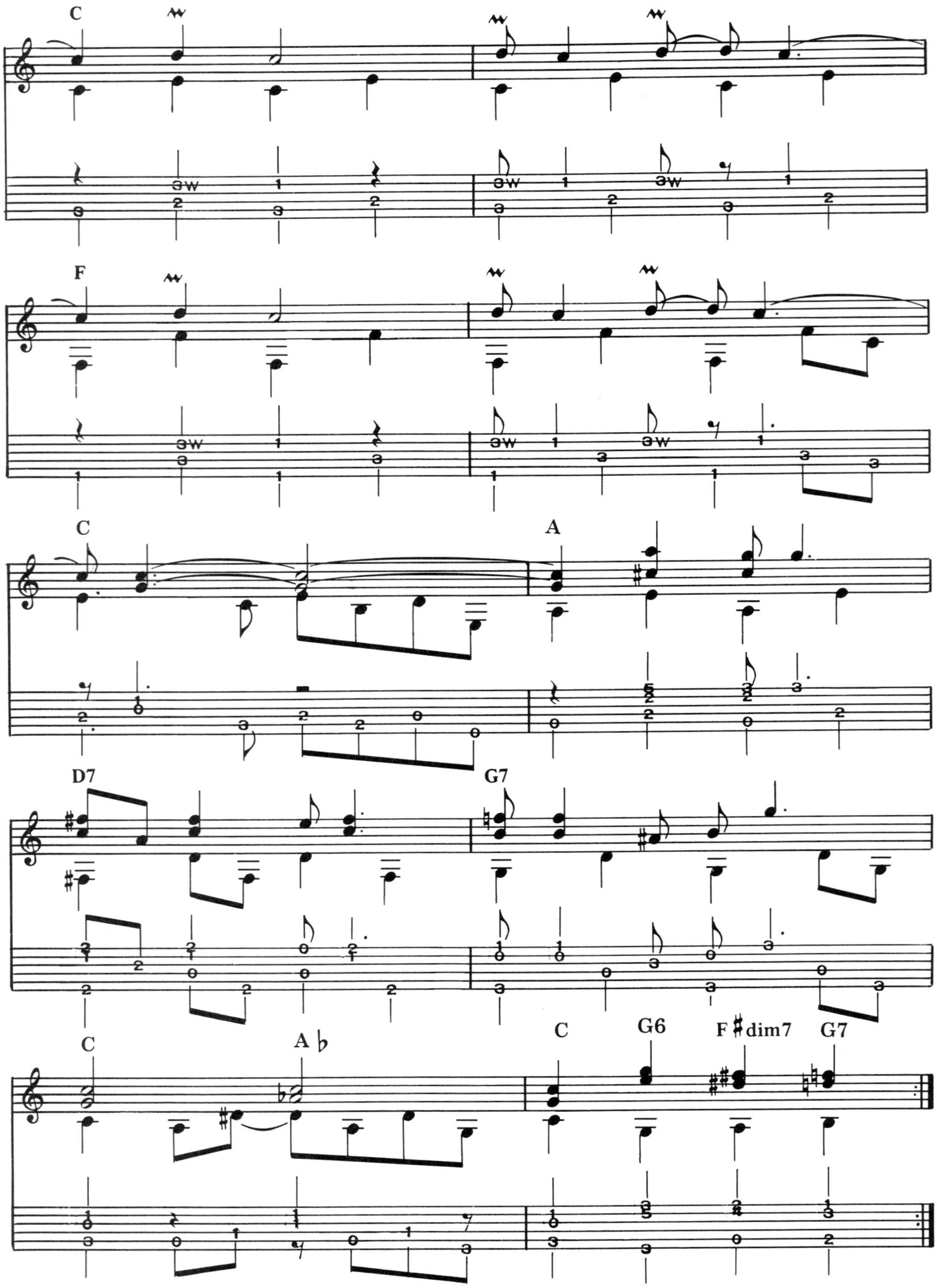
C
F
C
A
D7
G7
C
A ♭
C
G6
F ♯dim7
G7

Discography

A cassette that features all of
the material presented in this
volume is available from:
  Stefan Grossman's Guitar
  Workshop
  P.O. Box 804
  Cooper Station, N.Y. 10003

Blind Lemon Jefferson:
  "Prison Cell Blues"

The Immortal Blind Lemon Jefferson, Vol. 1
Milestone Records, 2004—and
American Folk Music Anthology, Vol. 3
Folkways Records, 2953

  "Easy Rider Blues"

The Immortal Blind Lemon Jefferson, Vol. 1
Milestone Records, 2004

William Moore:
  "One Way Gal"

Country Blues Encores
Origin Jazz Library, OJL-8

Blind Willie McTell:
  "Stole Rider Blues"

Ragtime Blues cassette available
from Stefan Grossman's Guitar
Workshop

*"Delia"
  ("All My Friends Are Gone")

Blind Willie McTell, 1940
Melodeon (Biograph) Records,
7323

* * *Blind Willie McTell*
Yazoo Records, 1005

* * *Blind Willie McTell, Vol. 2*
Yazoo Records, 1037

Blind Boy Fuller:
"Little Woman, You're So Sweet" — *Ragtime Blues* cassette available from Stefan Grossman's Guitar Workshop

"You've Got Something There" — *Blind Boy Fuller 1935-42* Blues Classics Records, 11 (Arhoolie)

"Piccolo Rag" — *Blind Boy Fuller, 1935-42* Blues Classics Records, 11 (Arhoolie)

"Careless Love" — *Blind Boy Fuller, 1935-42* Blues Classics Records, 11 (Arhoolie)

Big Bill Broonzy:
"Willie Mae" — *Blues* Folkways Records, 3817

"Shuffle Rag" — *Blues* Folkways Records, 3817

Sam McGee:
"Franklin Blues" — *Mr. Charlie's Blues* Yazoo Records, 1024

**Granddad of the Country Guitar Pickers* Arhoolie Records, 5012

Blind Lemon Jefferson:
"Rabbit Foot Blues" — *American Folk Music Anthology, Vol. 3* Folkways Records, 2953

"Hot Dogs" — *Texas-Arkansas-Louisiana Country* Yazoo Records, 1004

"Black Horse Blues" — *The Immortal Blind Lemon Jefferson, Vol. 1* Milestone Records, 2004

Blind Blake:
"Black Dog Blues" — *Blind Blake, Vol. 1* Biograph Records, 12003

"Policy Blues" — *Blind Blake, Vol. 1* Biograph Records, 12003

"That Will Never Happen No More" — *Blind Blake, Vol. 1* Biograph Records, 12003—and *The Georgia Blues* Yazoo Records, 1012

"Wabash Rag"

Guitar Wizards
Yazoo Records, 1016

"Police Dog Blues"

The Georgia Blues
Yazoo Records, 1012

"West Coast Blues"

Ragtime Blues cassette available
    from Stefan Grossman's Guitar
Workshop

*I have recorded "Delia" on
How to Play Blues Guitar, avail-
able from:
 Kicking Mule Records
 P.O. Box 3233
 Berkeley, California 94703

**These albums do not contain
any songs transcribed in this
book, but should be listened to
in order to understand the
styles of the musicians that
recorded them.

 You should try to keep on the
mailing lists of the following
companies as reissues continue
to appear that might be of great
value to you.

Arhoolie Records
P.O. Box 9195
Berkeley, California 94709

Biograph Records
1601 East 21st Street
Brooklyn, New York 11210

Blues Classics Records
c/o Arhoolie Records

Folkways Records
43 West 61st Street
New York, New York 10023

Milestone Records
22 East 48th Street
New York, New York 10017

Origin Jazz Library
P.O. Box 863
Berkeley, California 94701

Roots Records
Hauptstrasse
A 2371 Hinterbruhl
Austria

Roundup Records
P.O. Box 474
Somerville, Mass. 02144

Yazoo Records
245 Waverly Place
New York, New York 10014